DIASPORIC
VIETNAMESE
ARTISTS
NETWORK

ISABELLE THUY PELAUD AND VIET THANH NGUYEN
DVAN FOUNDERS

ALSO IN THE SERIES:

Constellations of Eve
Abbigail Nguyen Rosewood

Drowning Dragon Slips by Burning Plains: Poems
Khải Đơn

Hà Nội at Midnight: Stories
Bảo Ninh; translated and edited by Quan Manh Ha and Cab Tran

Longings: Contemporary Fiction by Vietnamese Women Writers
Translated by Quan Manh Ha and Quynh H. Vo

Nothing Follows
Lan P. Duong

*Watermark: Vietnamese American Poetry & Prose,
25th Anniversary Edition*
Edited by Barbara Tran, Monique Truong, and Khoi Luu

HAIR

A LAI MỸ MEMOIR

JADE HIDLE

TEXAS TECH UNIVERSITY PRESS

Copyright © 2025 by Jade Hidle

All rights reserved. No portion of this book may be reproduced in any form or by any means, including electronic storage and retrieval systems, except by explicit prior written permission of the publisher. Brief passages excerpted for review and critical purposes are excepted.

This book is typeset in EB Garamond. The paper used in this book meets the minimum requirements of ANSI/NISO Z39.48-1992 (R1997). ∞

Designed by Hannah Gaskamp
Cover designed by Hannah Gaskamp

Library of Congress Cataloging-in-Publication Data

Names: Hidle, Jade, 1983– author. Title: Hair: A Lai Mỹ memoir / Jade Hidle. Other titles: Lai Mỹ memoir. Description: Lubbock, Texas: Texas Tech University Press, [2025] | Series: Diasporic Vietnamese Artists Network (DVAN) | Summary: "A memoir featuring poems, essays, and letters to detail how mental health for Vietnamese Americans can be affected by family and cultural dynamics and societal issues"—Provided by publisher.
Identifiers: LCCN 2024057945 (print) | LCCN 2024057946 (ebook) |
ISBN 978-1-68283-249-3 (paperback) | ISBN 978-1-68283-250-9 (ebook)
Subjects: LCSH: Hidle, Jade, 1983– | Vietnamese American women—California, Southern—Biography. | Multiracial women—California, Southern—Biography. | Vietnamese Americans—California, Southern—Biography. | Multiracial people—California, Southern—Biography. | Vietnamese American women—Mental health—California, Southern. | Vietnamese Americans—Mental health—California, Southern. | California, Southern—Biography. | Compulsive hair pulling.
Classification: LCC F866.4.H54 A3 2025 (print) | LCC F866.4.H54 (ebook) |
DDC 305.8959/2207949092 [B]—dc23/eng/20250203
LC record available at https://lccn.loc.gov/2024057945
LC ebook record available at https://lccn.loc.gov/2024057946

Texas Tech University Press
Box 41037
Lubbock, Texas 79409-1037 USA
800.832.4042
ttup@ttu.edu
www.ttupress.org

For our children

"My sadness is an elongated state of emergency."
—Billy-Ray Belcourt

"they ask me to remember / but they want me to remember / their memories / and I keep on remembering / mine"
—Lucille Clifton

"It took many years of vomiting up all the filth I'd been taught about myself, and half-believed, before I was able to walk on the Earth as though I had a right to be here."
—James Baldwin

"Be who you are, even if it kills you. It will. Over and over again. Even as you live."
—Joy Harjo

CONTENTS

PROLOGUE:	THE ROOT	XI
CHAPTER 1:	"ME GOOK"	3
CHAPTER 2:	SONS OF NORWAY	13
	PHOTO ALBUM 1	17
CHAPTER 3:	GHOST STORIES	21
CHAPTER 4:	THE WHITE NBA	29
CHAPTER 5:	MS. ONO	33
CHAPTER 6:	DEAR RIDER STRONG	37
CHAPTER 7:	THÚY	43
CHAPTER 8:	PUPPETEER	55
	INTERLUDE-INTRUSION	61
CHAPTER 9:	PERIOD	63
CHAPTER 10:	THERAPIST 1	67
	INTERLUDE-INTRUSION	69
CHAPTER 11:	THERAPIST 2	71
CHAPTER 12:	TROLL	75
	PHOTO ALBUM 2	91
CHAPTER 13:	SLEEPER	95
CHAPTER 14:	THE CHRISTIAN AND THE QUAIL	109
CHAPTER 15:	DEAR ANGELINA JOLIE	115

CONTENTS

CHAPTER 16: THERAPIST 4 — **123**
    INTERLUDE-INTRUSION — 125
CHAPTER 17: "UNDERCOVER GOOK" — **127**
CHAPTER 18: HOT DOGS — **139**
CHAPTER 19: DIEM, THE TAILOR — **149**
    PHOTO ALBUM 3 — 161
CHAPTER 20: LETTER TO A MỸ LAI MOTHER — **165**
CHAPTER 21: THERAPIST 6 AND THE ANTEATER — **179**
    INTERLUDE-INTRUSION — 183
CHAPTER 22: THE WIG — **185**
CHAPTER 23: CRADLE CAP — **191**
    PHOTO ALBUM 4 — 195
CHAPTER 24: THE SUM OF DIRT — **197**
CHAPTER 25: DEAR ZACHARY LEVI — **205**
    INTERLUDE-INTRUSION — 219
    EPILOGUE: PUSH — **221**

ACKNOWLEDGMENTS — **235**
PREVIOUS PUBLICATION VENUES — **239**

PROLOGUE: THE ROOT

As I'm writing this to you, I'm thinking of something else. I always am.

If I wasn't always indexing my hair's different colors and textures, I would be clear-headed enough to think of more beautiful sentences. If my fingers weren't magnetically drawn to the coarsest hairs and, later, the whitest hairs, then my hands would be typing more words for you to read, to understand. Then maybe you wouldn't ask, "What are you?" and then see my face and question, "What's wrong?" only to really wonder, "What happened to your hair?" Then I wouldn't have to see you staring at my patchy scalp while I struggle to answer your first question with percentages and hyphens. If I wasn't chronically compelled to self-inflict the pain of ripping my hair roots from scalp—the wet popping of release—then, maybe, like Jo March's words that punctured my heart, "I should have been a great many things."

What scientist or traveler I wish I could have been if I were a free body, not trussed by twine of sadness and chronic suicidal thoughts and the minute-to-minute intrusive, obsessive thoughts about my hair. Tug. Pluck. Hide. Grow. Sort. Divide. Isolate. Pull. Rip. Count. Save and save and lose and remember and want and grieve. The compulsion is relentless. It is the mental version of my mother's pinch choking my nose, suffocating all those other rivulets of blood and potential, shriveling in and picking at itself—lash after lash, root after root from this skin without a chance—like a shore in fast-forward erosion, like an incessant making of death.

PROLOGUE: THE ROOT

One of the things she taught me that my body will never forget is that cutting our hair is part of letting go—to mourn a death, to sweep away a year gone. It feels true that pulling hair is grieving in perpetuity. It feels true that hairpulling is a way to wear my unbelonging. It feels true that, as a daughter of diaspora surviving in empire, I might always be running but am never able to outrun grief.

When they found the mummy of mother and child in Lemon Grove, California, scientists and spectators exclaimed that the preserved strands of dried hair made her look so alive. But when the wind blows my remaining combed-over strands and reveals the bald patches that my calloused plucking fingers fly quickly to cover, you will worry and wonder about how close to dead I look.

Is it cancer? Alopecia? "Did you get that postpartum hair loss?" a woman in the pediatrician's waiting room asked. "No," I said. "What is your worst health problem?"

The tangling of life and death is not so foreign to me. I can't remember a time in my life that I didn't think that I would be better off dead. Bụi đời, "dust of life," was the term for mixed-race Vietnamese kids like me who were assumed products of American GIs and Vietnamese sex workers. No one ever said that phrase so directly, but I could see in their faces, cringing around their words, that they were channeling its spirit. Learning that my mother was Vietnamese and my father a white American, assumptions were made, and their eyes waned with the association of my life with a history of war overflowing with so much death. Just as the wind scatters the seeds in diaspora, wind also blows the dust of life, bụi đời—the mixed children of shame, of life and death muddled—these are the scattered words that fall into some story of me, a lai Mỹ girl, first in her family born in the States, but who carries things, who rips out the lashes meant to keep dust out of the eyes, and who writes words about it.

The doctors' word for it is trichotillomania. The Greek etymology of the term stems from Aristotle's writing about hairpulling. Before that, pulling out a body's hair was part of intricate funeral rituals in Egypt. Across the Atlantic, the indigenous Amazonian Ticuna tribe performed the coming-of-age ceremony, pelazón, in which girls are ushered into adolescence with a communal pulling of all their hair—a death of girlhood and regrowth into womanhood. When the prophet Nehemiah pulled his hair out in response to one of the many tragedies in the Bible, idioms about "tearing my hair out" mushroomed across geography, cultures, and languages. I can't count how many times my body has tensed up when a stressed coworker or annoyed friend casually uses the phrase, only to realize they haven't yet noticed that I am an actual, chronic hair puller.

Growing up, I did not hear a Vietnamese word for trichotillomania. When I search for "hairpulling" in Vietnamese all of the results are advertisements for spas. Typical.

But I have absorbed a lexicon of judgment for being all varieties of words with that throat-scraping spit of the Klingon-like aspirated "k"—"khùng," "khó ưa," "khó chịu"—and, of course, incessant critiques of my body, including my hair. Given that the ob-gyn was apparently playing it loose and casual during my mother's ultrasound appointments, I was predicted to be a boy. The piles of blue and yellow clothes gifted at my baby shower led people to read my prolonged baby baldness as male gender identity. Following suit, I was a kid "so big" or "fat," "too dark," with a trán dô and nose that was "bự quá!"—all excess. From birth, I was "so bald" until I was two. When hair eventually grew in enough to fulfill the Asian child milestone of a bowl cut, my family members sighed in relief that the crisp bangs covered my fivehead. "Trán dô" was my nickname. It was the only Vietnamese phrase my dad ever learned. "Tan yo," he laughed. "You got a big head from me." When puberty hit early and fast, the Vietnamese women who raised me coveted-critiqued my height, breasts, and heavy dark eyelashes and chestnut hair. My mother often showed her love for me, as well as her hatred for herself, by saying, "I want to pull off your hair and wear it."

Vietnamese hair, I think, is admired: straight, black, smooth. But that, like every fetish, is an incomplete picture. My mom complained about the natural darkness and coarseness of her hair that many people in the world paid top dollar for, and she held up to my hair boxes of chestnut-mahogany-mushroom-medium-rich-other-marketing-terms-for-brown-hair dye, seeking a perfect match. The jealousy, the competition, was built into our DNA. Everything that I was pained her for what she was not. I was guilty. I was guilty of hurting her just by being alive. Tangled in my guilt was the shame of being born in the US, of knowing who my father was, of going to school, of playing with dolls, of being a living reminder of everything she didn't have. If my very body inflicted pain upon her, I would destroy it. In this way, hairpulling was my manifestation of attempting to remove this competition, this deep-seeded pain, from our relationship—to rip it from its roots.

Words I *do* know in Vietnamese are the words for "to write" (viết) and "to kill" (giết). Their sonic similarity, though, hinges upon a Southern accent. In the Vietnamese classes I've taken, it seems a consensus that those from the Southern part of Việt Nam, where my family is from, speak fast and loose, a little drrrty. While it's true that the mother tongue I grew up hearing and speaking is the muddy boondocks "may-tao" roll, colonialism's reach is far. Someone told my mom who told me to use "Mẹ" instead of "Má" and to pronounce "viết" (to write) with a "v" instead of the "g" that sounds like "y." All of these substitutions.

I made the mistake of pronouncing the "v" in front of some first-generation South Vietnamese boys from the San Gabriel Valley. "Oooohhh weee, điệu quá! You some kind of sympathizer, em ơi?"

I mumbled an excuse about my mẹ going to French Catholic school and laughed it off. At home, I recited all the "v" words I knew—"vội," "vớ," "vàng," "vui"—and practiced pronouncing them in an "authentic" Southern Vietnamese dialect. I hoped that bringing "viết" and "giết" together would mean writing about it could kill the hairpulling problem. Maybe it would finally release the urge to pull and blink out like a black hole, the inheritance to which my body responded louder than words. Maybe it would be as described by Virginia Woolf, the writer in whom I found a mother I needed, in my favorite of her novels, *To the Lighthouse* (its multiple references to "little Chinese eyes" attest to how racism is inescapable, even in the things we love): "in expressing it I explained it and then laid it to rest." I worry that doing so will also end up killing my mother and all that she is to my identity. I worry that I am killing myself but am compelled to do so anyway. "I no longer hear her voice; I do not see her," Woolf wrote.

From womb to womb of multiple generations of women, I inherited the sugared blood that makes me unquenchably thirsty, a liver hot and hard

PROLOGUE: THE ROOT

with the incurable "-itis," and a heart like the ones who loved me first that palpitates until I choke on my own breath. Perhaps, too, I inherited the hairpulling. My mother once said she did the same as a girl and that was why her lashes became so short and thin. "Like me," she said and laughed, reciting her story about a monk telling her that her firstborn child—me— would be her shadow. She claimed each of my struggles and wounds as her own. I resisted believing that she was a hairpuller too, mostly because I was hurt that she continued to look at herself instead of me.

The only other time she addressed my hairpulling directly was when she offered to beat my hands with chopsticks every time she noticed me plucking. With every flu and fever, she had taken care of me with Sprite, rice porridge, steaming pots of Chinese herbal medicine, and cạo gió (coining my back to "catch the bad wind"), but she did not know how to take care of this kind of sick. "No, thank you," I said, surely hurting her again with this rejection of painful love.

A generation back, my bà ngoại, tuned into another time, slept in small spurts throughout the day and night. Oftentimes, she floated in some liminal zone between sleeping and waking. Either she lay on her back with her feet planted so her knees windshield-wipered to the same rhythm that her palm or forearm rubbed her forehead—xoa, xoa—as if to smooth away the memories that furrowed her brow; or, she sat on the couch, arms limp palms up on her thighs as she swayed an endless circle. An insomniac myself, I peered from behind doorframes or chairs to watch her. The swaying and her indecipherable mumbling were hypnotic. The rhythm was only broken by her hand slapping a peeling Salonpas back into place on her forehead, neck, or shoulders.

Just as deeply as she was in it, she would break from it, quickly and urgently. She rustled in her plastic bags of drugstore perfume and her Tamagotchi-like glucometer with pinprick needles for prescription pills rattling in their sick urine-orange bottles. Once she found what she was swallowing into her next nap, she groomed. From her permed crisp hair, like Top Ramen pre-boil, she removed the intricate system of cross-hatched bobby pins and scattered them on the table with her labyrinth of used toothpicks and peeled Salonpas patches. She then took an afro pick to rake her peeking scalp and puff the remnants of what, in the '60s, was a silken upward cascade of beehive that rivaled those of Ronnie Spector and The Shangri-Las sisters. "Make bigger," she'd say at once to herself and to me.

In its many iterations, my bà ngoại's hair was resistance too. She was doing different than her mother. My great-grandmother had grown her hair to her knees, but you never would have known it because she wore it in a bun—that is, until the day she shaved it off to mourn her husband who would accompany the ghost of her twin that she fought with a kitchen knife.

Maybe my bà ngoại knew from her travels on other timelines that I, with my flat hair, would need to be reminded to resist shrinking, to take up space by believing I deserved it. To "make bigger" my self.

But this will not be the story of the traumas suffered and survived by my mother and grandmother and great-grandmother and all the ancestors preceding her on our matrilineal branches. This is not one of the epic stories that wins prizes. In the stacks of handwritten letters that my mother has slipped under my door throughout my childhood, I have been reminded, warned, threatened that her stories—stories of Việt Nam—are not mine because I am not not not. Her line-packing scrawl hinged upon my lack and deficiency, tumbled out of my being an absence, and every word she added reminded me that I was a negative, a taking away. In her truth, I was not simply at zero. I was in debt. She reminded me, in a story I carry within me to this day, that everyone wanted to abort me, except for her. I was meant to die, but, she wrote, she saved me because she loved me more than anyone else could. For that, I was in her debt. Accordingly, she slipped these letters under my door and relied on my silence. She never brought up the issues in her letter once she had delivered it; doing so would have offered me the opportunity to respond. Her letters, and later her emails and text messages, were meant to be the final word.

I never asked anyone to verify her abortion story. That answer didn't matter so much as the fact that a story lives on in the way that it was used, the way it made me feel. As Maya Angelou said, "I've learned that people will forget what you said, people will forget what you did, but people will never forget how you made them feel." I could never forget that my indebted birth laid the foundation for an internal colonialism. Mimi Thi Nguyen wrote about how Vietnamese Americans are cast as indebted to the US for gifting them freedom and a new home; part of the obligatory repayment was to tell a rags-to-riches story that made a "good refugee." Even more indebted were the mixed kids like me "saved" from a country that punished them. As if hate had borders. It was inside. And this internalized sense of debt would not, could not, be answered with linear stories, percentages, and awards. I did not offer the expected responses to recurring questions. I was—we were—a war that could not be won. Truths twisted.

My mother was the one who coached me to remain strategically silent and to lie about my ethnicity (French), my age (discounts), her age (youth), the year she came to the US (the Việt Cộng are always watching), how much money she had or didn't have (shoeboxes), what she did or didn't say about my dad (everything), and so many other things that I grew anxious about keeping them straight. Paralyzed, I opted to stay quiet.

Quiet didn't help. I embarrassed her. Are you "dumb"? "Retarded"? Or just "rude"? "Why can't you bow? Say something, anything better than sitting silent like you hate being here. What is so bad about your life that your face is always một đống?"

I was the pendulum swinging between not enough and too much.

Her words echo in my head daily. I cannot remember a time when her words were not the language with which I conceived of and spoke to myself: Liar. Traitor. Disappointment. Look at yourself. Look.

I have always defended and excused my mother, even to myself, in hopes of being accepted by her. I've fractioned myself further with every apology. I now understand that acceptance is not possible. There is only the practice of writing, of keeping the keys clicking louder to edge out her creeping voice that puppeteers my plucking hands. The writing is my attempt to kill it. You must understand that this will be my symbolic murder. The truth is the way I stay alive for you.

All bones look similar, but it's the muscles that tell the story. I shrink and pull and knot to contort like a shrimp caving from within, boiled tighter and paler, that shit line darkening through my skin that bears the pull and punch of cycling memory, that lifts in laughter but falls harder. The doctors agree that the pain is pain—not just me—and it is chronic. Every morning

PROLOGUE: THE ROOT

the right side of my body aches as if I was beaten throughout the night. The nausea and stabs send my stomach into unpredictable yet certain tides of diarrhea and constipation, of hunger and revulsion. Migraines sear from eye sockets shooting to the back of my head and nerves pinch along my neck, around my right shoulder blade, and all the way down to my fingertips that buzz then numb. My throat constricts because a shrimp cannot swallow so much ocean.

> "The sea was more important now than the shore. Waves were all round them, tossing and sinking, with a log wallowing down one wave; a gull riding on another. About here, she thought, dabbling her fingers in the water, a ship had sunk, and she murmured dreamily half asleep, how we perished, each alone" (Woolf 191).

All of it, blood or epigenetic, is what neuroscientists attribute to the vagus nerve, which when overactivated by trauma results in chronic health problems and pain, as well as cognitive emergency states such as hypervigilance. The Terminator's point of view captured how my mind works: infrared radars constantly scanning and assessing, tracking every detail as a potential threat. When it came to my hair, I was Series 800, Model 101, in distinguishing hairs, mentally cataloging them based on their color, level of sun bleaching, texture, length, and the promise of pain that I felt as I lightly tugged near the root. Isolating that pain to the pinprick of a hair root numbed all the rest. I was paralyzed by plucking, and sometimes hours passed in a haze and pile of hair sticky with wet roots.

The silence, and staring, and slouching made others, not just my mother, assume I was dumb or indifferent or just a straight-up bitch, but these dissociative periods are actually when I am deep in a very alive body that has not been abused by others and myself. I am somewhere else—Santorini or Cork or Santiago, always a coastline—where I am unthinking all the things I overthink, especially my hair. The sun is warm on my skin and patchy eyelids and scalp, regenerating the hair with ancient magic like Anne Rice's mummies. I can see them, like a reverse x-ray, darkening through the tapestry of vessels in my eyelids when I close my eyes. I fantasize about my body melding with nature so that my mind is not thinking of my hair because my body is not just my own but part of a larger system that grows and heals faster than it destroys.

As much as I was addicted to the pulling, I was hooked on the healing too. Post-pluck, I obsessively iced puffy eyelids and swabbed warm water and, desperately, milk on bloody, itchy lashlines. I scraped salmon skin with my teeth to swallow all of the fatty gray chunks whose omega-3s offered a natural promise of beating depression and regrowing hair. When I moved to pulling the hair on my head because of the promise of more hair that wouldn't be as noticeable if I plucked, I was disappointed to witness that I simply just pulled more, and I attempted to console myself by meticulously applying series of minty shampoos, burning sprays, and tingling creams to the exposed patches of my waxen scalp. I drank mushroom teas in hopes that the earthen flavor would not just regrow the hairs but open up parts of my brain that had locked pain deep inside. When I've wanted nothing more than to die because I looked and felt that way anyway, what kept me alive is this insistence to heal.

Despite the fact that I've lived triple the number of years in pain than not, I've clung to possibility. After decades of sloppily and shamefully cutting my own hair, I crave the sensation of a hairstylist washing my scalp or my husband stroking my hair without my whole body tensing over the fear that my hair would make them more uncomfortable than it already makes me. I crave the touch and tingle that would assure me that this is my body and that my body is me. As a người lai Mỹ, people are always telling me I'm not who I look like or they don't even know what I look like—a reminder that I will never belong in the body that I'm in.

Despite this lack of control of my body that rips itself harder than everyone else, there is an eclipse-thin ring of light that promises some somatic healing, even if just a step or two in my body without the glare of acute awareness that I bear visual evidence of my defenselessness against my inheritance. The ties come undone momentarily when you reach for me or touch me in the way that I am reassured is not to inflict pain. The momentary loosening is warm and I can feel it tingle from scalp to shins. In this feeling glows the promise of breaking legacies of invisibility.

I am slowly learning how to rest from harming myself, envisioning a prawn supine and twisting and unfurling antennae and claws, flinging the

PROLOGUE: THE ROOT

deceptive weight of water skyward. The drips, all these crystalline memories of the shrimp I've been, cling to the ceiling. And wait. But falling water is clean. It becomes nourishment. You are chạo tôm, formed on sugar cane, then sliced free.

HAIR

CHAPTER 1

"ME GOOK"

Save for the every-other-weekend visits to my dad, I lived with my mom in an indistinguishable apartment within rows of indistinguishable buildings for people who had been rendered indistinguishable. Most of our neighbors were recent immigrants from Mexico.

We were living away from home in San Pedro, between our apartment in "affordable housing units for low-income families in transition" (read: the projects) and my grandparents' house in the suburban hills of that class-tiered city. The geography was advantageous for segregation. Gaffey Street, the main artery of Pedro bustling with all the fast food joints and every other business you'd need, divided the green arc of the Vincent Thomas Bridge (off of which so many people died, my mother reminded me every time we drove over it), the ports and their Lego-stacked cargo containers, and the downtown area from the residential neighborhoods, which ascended in class status as they did in elevation. The white girls from school lived on the hilltops; they always had new clothes and backpacks not just every year, but every season, and their family names appeared on real estate signs. The mid-level hills were middle-class suburban where my grandparents lived on my grandfather's military pension. The projects where my mother and I lived sloped down one of Pedro's long, steep hills, and the

CHAPTER 1

identical buildings multiplied in rows that seemed to continue endlessly down the hill, past where I could see, let alone travel by rollerblades or my scuffed-up saddle shoes. What I do remember of daily life in the projects was mariachi music cut with the man ringing the bell on his paleta cart and the sounds of the children who followed him.

During the summer of 1992, the tension of the LA Riots still burned in our neighborhood. While the news focused on Rodney King and, to a lesser degree, violence between Black and Korean people, there were gunshots whose stories did not get told. That summer, a group of men opened fire on the school that was at the foot of the development. I peered out of our doorway and watched as teenage boys from our buildings, some from different gangs, emerged from their apartments with guns and bats in tow, holding up their sagging pants as they ran, together, toward the school.

On my elbows and knees, I tried to keep our boys (I didn't know them but wanted to belong to them and them to us in this moment of fighting) in sight by inching across the threshold until only my toes remained in the apartment, as if this would appease my mother's orders to stay inside no matter what until she came home from work. Quickly their figures shrank and disappeared, so I curled up in the doorway and strained my ears for voices or shots. All I heard was Sylvia's unmistakable raspy growl that sounded like, by nine years old, she had fought in World War II and smoked three million cigarettes. "Hey, puta, they're coming for you."

I looked up and saw her peering down at me from her second-story apartment landing.

Though Sylvia was nine like me, her face looked like the "after" photo in a true Hollywood story about some telenovela starlet gone bad, but with a smirk that still made her seem better than everyone else. "That's not funny, Sylvia."

"Oh, are you scared?"

"Aren't you?"

Sylvia licked chili powder from her palm. "No. Cuz I'm not a puta Chino, puta Chino."

I sighed. "Is Claudia home?"

"ME GOOK"

She was lying on her back now, so all I could see were her arms and legs air-conducting the rhythm to her song, "Ching chong ching ching chong..."

I shut the door and sat by the window to wait for my mother to come home.

Sylvia was the mischievous half of Wanda's pair of daughters. With her sweet sister Claudia, I often spent weekend and summer afternoons on the landing of their staircase. I rarely went inside their apartment because, though I wanted to, I felt it was some kind of unspoken trespass, a betrayal of my mother. Out on the landing, Claudia and I ate uncooked Top Ramen and coconut paletas as our mothers worked, and Sylvia ran throughout the development bartering Mexican candies for makeup and money.

I liked Wanda because she didn't pretend. She responded to Sylvia's sass with stronger sass. With Claudia and me, Wanda was always tender and generous, so it felt like validation that I was good. This was validation I craved. "Hi, Ha-day," Wanda greeted me. "Mom," Claudia groaned. "It's not Ha-day. It's Jade. Jay-Duh."

"Oh jes, okay, I say Jay-Duh. You learn so much at school, Claudia. Much better than Mami." She covertly pressed into Claudia's palm change for paletas while Sylvia wasn't looking and, turning to me, said, "One for you too, Ha-Day."

"Mom!"

"Okay, okay!" As she left for work, she patted the tops of our heads with a "mija"—a term of endearment, yes, but also a promise.

"I don't get why Dylan even likes Brenda," Claudia said to me one evening as we sat on the steps of our building. "She's kind of a . . ." Claudia paused to see if her mom was in earshot. "A bitch."

I nodded and licked the last of the chicken-flavored powder from my palm. Dusk had fallen and moths began to circle and bump their fuzzy heads against the lamp above us. Being outside in the darkness excited me, more so because I got to listen to Claudia, three years older than me, reflect on how on-screen relationships were panning out.

CHAPTER 1

The whiteness of my mother's nursing uniform took shape as she approached the stairs. I stuffed my empty candy wrappers into my back pocket. "Hello, Miss," Claudia said. "Wow, you getting so big," my mother replied. Claudia tugged at the hem of her t-shirt.

"Chay," my mother said to me. She had chosen for me a name that my father would be able to pronounce but whose "j" and middle-of-the-word "d" weren't natural to her native tongue. To become "more American," my mother had sacrificed her ability to call her firstborn by name. Mẹ blamed the humidity of my August birthday for her haphazard naming: "Dey ask, ask, ask me but so hot I jus look aroun and see my bracelet. Okay, I say, Chay!" She and I have rituals for these retellings, so I always replied, "If you had looked around the hospital room, I could have been named 'I.V.' or 'bed pan' or 'big nurse shoe'?" I could rely on her half-smile, tongue-click, and then, "So stupid! Okay, shut up, you distract me!" She shooed me away while calling me back: "I not done with the story yet."

"In Việt Nam," as was often her way of launching into a story, "old people wear to keep their body warm. See?" She jiggled her wrist and the jade bracelet spun. "It change color because it change with the body." On the day we met, that day she named me, my growth intersected with her growth and, so, I am born to care for her every time I write it, every time she called for me, "Chay, ơi" instead of Ngọc Bích, the name for every beautiful Viet girl I've envied, wanting to be the unmixed daughter I could never be. Once I dared to ask her, "Why didn't you name me Ngọc instead?"

"Oh yeah," my mẹ sputtered sarcastically, "because America know how to say that." I mouthed my lost name, lips softly cupping.

"Chay, ơi, let's go to store."

"Okay." I knew the tone in her voice, a tangling of fatigue and the ever-present sadness, so I would say yes to whatever she wanted. "Bye, Claudia," I said. She waved good-bye to me as she took the rest of the stairs up to the open door of her apartment where Wanda was laughing at something on one of the Spanish-language channels.

We moved through the aisles according to routine, by memory, collecting the bare essentials for only the next two days or so, which was as far as we could look ahead back then. Plus, because food was love (at least until

"ME GOOK"

it was eaten and then became shame), my mom treated me to a Sara Lee frozen poundcake. After shopping, my mom dropped me off in front of the building to take up the groceries that needed refrigerating while she went to search for a parking space. As I was putting the milk away and peeling the soggy receipt from the side of the jug, a police-style pounding shook the door in its frame. I hesitated and listened, approaching the door only when I heard Wanda's voice on the other side, yelling, "Ha-day, open! Ha-day! Why do you do this locking the door? Come!" When I unlocked and opened the door, she grabbed my hand and dragged me down the stairs, the soles of my bare feet scratching against the concrete. As soon as the street came into view, I saw my mother's peach Ford station wagon spun diagonally across the lane lines, the exhaust smoking over a spray of shattered glass.

Closer, I could see my mother inside, her head cocked back against the headrest as if she had fallen asleep. Suddenly, Wanda looked at my bare feet and grunted "Ay!" and nestled her hands under my arms to lift me across the broken glass to my mother.

"Mom," I said. She moaned and her left shoulder twitched against the crushed door. I could feel Wanda's knee push up against my butt to hold me there. "See, mija, she's okay," Wanda said.

"Mom," I called, and I remember thinking that her eyeliner made it look like someone had painted her eyes shut. Wanda's chest, heaving with breath, pressed into my back.

As the sirens approached, Wanda began to pull me away, but I grasped my mother's unresponsive face and became nervous about how soft her skin felt. *Be stronger*, I remember thinking. Wanda whispered "Ha-day, mija," her aspirations warm and light against my left temple, and I let go.

It wasn't until years later that I learned that, on the Mohs scale, jadeite—solidified by iron and interlocking crystals—ranks at a 7 out of 10. It dares stone carvers to leave their mark, rotating metal spikes—what look like instruments of torture—to etch the most delicate details into jade. In our homelands before borders, jade became what we needed: feeding to killing to honoring. Olmec and Maya masks, plaques, and figures in jade mimic the hues of flickering scales shedding in rebirth, becoming what artists dreamed: the salivary shine of opium pipe mouthpieces, warriors'

CHAPTER 1

pounamu medallions, the four-ton Buddha circumnavigating to kneeling hopeseekers cast in her green glow. It was for jade's strength and durability that Han kings and queens demanded crafting burial suits to protect their journeys to immortality from life's demons and ghosts.

So, maybe, at the risk of being unable to call me, my mother named me to make me hard, strong.

As my mother recovered from the hit-and-run accident, her frailty underscored my obligation to please her. So I did whatever she wanted. To prove to her I was good. Strong.

One other Asian family lived at the end of the hall. But they were Korean. When we passed by them in the hall with groceries, my mom nodded out of obligation to our internalized hierarchy of Asian countries that ranked Koreans well above us because of their cars, light skin, and beauty products and plastic surgery. This particular Korean family reinforced our inferiority complex. They had a dad. His voice came from low within him like distant thunder. During a failed playdate, I witnessed the two sisters pray and do homework in quiet except for the occasional squeak on their plastic-draped furniture. (They were clean, unlike me who'd just had lice that my mom squeezed off my scalp until her fingertips were spotted with louse blood.) The father diaphragm-bellowed an invitation for me to stay for dinner, and the vibration of this paternal voice made me nod my head, even though I didn't want to stay. Mẹ prepared me to visit the Han apartment by ponytailing my hair so tight it felt like it made my eyes slant, all while reminding me to be on my best behavior with Koreans. "Say thank you," she urged, but I mostly apologized. I broke unspoken rules about coasters, chopstick etiquette, and the Christian prayer to bless the food laid out across their carved wooden table. In our own apartment, Mẹ and I usually sat cross-legged on the carpet to eat at the coffee table while learning slang from *90210* and *Melrose Place*.

After dinner, I speed-slunk back to our apartment. "You see what kind cream the mother use? Shiseido? Korean so light skin."

"No," I responded to the silence between us where the promise of moving up the Asian ladder by association used to be. She sniffed my head, and for a moment I hoped for a Vietnamese kiss, but instead, "Stink." I trudged to the bathroom.

As if in consolation, Mẹ followed me and lowered her voice to the gossip octave. According to the ladder, Koreans, though as cold and calculating as their cheekbones were sharp, were still trailing behind the Japanese and Chinese. It was its own kind of twist that I could feel how much my mother loved me in the moments that she was badmouthing entire cultures to make me feel better. I was taught that gossip, secrecy, and lies were the ways to closeness. It's oftentimes been hard to trace a line between myself and the person rendered by the gossip. And I have been the most common subject. I've never been more cruel to anybody than I have been to myself.

This internal fight was just one bristle of the broom. Some Vietnamese had gossiped to me their blame of Korean mercenary soldiers during the US war in Việt Nam for profiting from betraying their own kind. In this instance, Vietnamese and Koreans were one. After all, Americans had mistaken us for each other as they called us both "gook." But that was only because US soldiers had misinterpreted "miguk," which translated from Korean meant "beautiful country," yet was used to refer to "America," and then wielded to Other. The word testified to the division underlying whatever fleeting alliance we might have wanted to forge. We mistook that we could come together in America, in that apartment building, through "me, gook." But we were not the same kind of Asian.

We dangled from our low rung of the Asian ladder the night that I returned from the Han family's apartment. My mother and I slept side by side. When I requested that she stroke my hair until I could fall asleep, she laughed that I was spoiled but still did it anyway. It was her way of saying "yes" when she was used to "no." It was one of the moments that I felt her love for me and, even though I didn't want it to end, I fell asleep because it was always easier knowing she was still awake. Maybe it was her touch that passed it on to me. I was a bedwetter. My diaper crinkled when I turned toward the wall to force away nightmares about being paralyzed and unable to save my mother as a young girl. I dreamed of crushed and popped bodies,

CHAPTER 1

hurtling meteors, fires and drowning, and, in the wee morning stages of my deep unconsciousness, drowning in feces, blood, and urine.

I slept.

I peed in our shared bed.

The cold of my exposed wet legs woke me in the morning.

Through gooey eyes, I saw my mother laughing and holding up our blanket as a magician does with a tablecloth. She pointed at my diaper and said, "See?" It was then that I noticed she was talking to the Han sisters. And Sylvia. They had been invited. Gossip was closeness. Now with someone else. The Han sisters and Sylvia stared in silence.

The sheets and my mom's clothing were soaked. I pulled a pillow over my cold, wet lower body and slunk to the bathroom, reaching to overhear what my mom was saying to the Han sisters as she walked them down the hall. "She can't play with you today. Too bad. You don't pee in your bed, huh?" Their collective "no" faded down the hallway until I heard our front door click locked behind them.

She had jeopardized an opportunity for me to form a stronger connection with the level-up Koreans in order to expose me. I wasn't brave enough to ask "why?" but my paralyzed silence said as much.

In response, she recounted a story I had heard before and that I would hear again, multiple times. "When I was your age, my grandma strip my clothes and beat me in the street where the whole neighborhood could see. 'Their eyes will make you remember not to make this mistake again' my grandma say."

As with all of my mother's stories about the war and immigration and Việt Nam in general, my imagination confronted its threshold. All I could do was emotionally shudder, afraid and grieving for my traumatized girl-mother. I tried to understand, and was desperate to forgive, how her pain was so great that she couldn't help but inflict it on me too. I was trying, struggling. But on the outside, I could tell by how she looked at me, I was impassive and vacant. I had to be. I had to freeze my body while transported to this place and time that had seized my mother and now was part of me even though I'd never been. The frenetic coursing of here and there, now and then, her and me—it was all shelled in the glazed-over vessel that was my body. My disassociation made her feel, I can only imagine, more unseen, more alone. She'd try to crack me by asking why I was dumb. How could I be so unfeeling? This time, though, she said, "What I do to you is not so bad. Not the end of the world. Say 'thank you.'"

CHAPTER 2

SONS OF NORWAY

Norway is called the "land of the midnight sun" because at certain times of year its proximity to the Arctic Circle bleeds sunset into sunrise. The day simultaneously changes and never ends. This is where my paternal grandfather is from. This is why my dad has a Viking's name. This is why the fjord-floating island is named after us—or, rather, our big-palmed, long-earlobed Viking ancestors farming that bit of rock in the middle of a cold sea. This is why even this little Vietnamese girl got invited to the Christmas parties thrown by the Sons of Norway.

The organization as it is today offers cultural resources such as recipes and language instruction, as well as scholarships and grants—you know, all the things that Norway is so popular for.

But in 1989, to me, Sons of Norway was a mansion overlooking the bluffs on Ocean Boulevard in Long Beach. It had a name: Wuthering Heights. The Norwegians boasted that W. C. Fields had once lived there, and I knew from the thrust of their voices that this was a piece of Hollywood. This was not just the rich my mom called my dad because he was white. *This* was

CHAPTER 2

movie rich. But it wasn't until I saw the daughter's bedroom that I truly felt the chasm of difference between this Daughter of Norway's life and mine in the buildings that had lots of words—low-income housing development for families in transition—but no names. My school didn't even get named after a colonial figure from US history. It was just "7th Street School."

The Norwegian girl's hair was so blonde it was white, and her dresses were frilly and from department stores. Her room was a renovated attic with a spire, like a castle. Like in fairy tales that can only be drawn. The rounded walls of her room were lined with custom-built shelves, each one the size of a stable for a My Little Pony. With a Vanna White–like sweep of her arm, she showcased the cinematically massive collection of plastic horses with cute stamps on their scented haunches. The other girlchildren and I stared, mouths gaping.

This rich girl knew she had us where she wanted us. She pulled Cupcake off of its shelf and, with its tiny hairbrush, stroked its long golden mane. "Good girl, Cupcake," she cooed. Then to us, "You can look, but don't touch any of my ponies. I don't want them to get dirty."

In that moment, this Norwegian princess positioned me as less important than a plastic horse, not even the prettiest one. The ice-cream-green body that gave Minty her name put Cupcake's trite pinkness to shame. I could see her beckoning to me from a high shelf. She reminded me of the halved girl in the afterlife waiting room in *Beetlejuice*: magnetic. But I would never even be able to touch Minty. "Don't sit on that," the princess barked at me. "You'll break it!"

I was one of those Norway-imported trolls from downstairs where the adults were. Dark and grotesque and protruding in all the wrong places, I retreated from the high tower's glow of Equestria magic, back downstairs where I belonged hovering around tables of lutefisk and meatballs and marzipan fruits that filled old seamen bellies until they groaned, "Uff da."

A band of sweet old ladies who smelled like Christmas and cats cornered me: "What's your name? . . . Oh, how exotic!"

"Elskling, where is your mother? . . . Well, you must get your color from her."

"Do you know how to say— . . . No?"

"Are you— . . . Okay, kjære, you don't have to say. Have you tried the marzipan?"

The almond paste was grainy, and the edible paint that made it look like fruit gave it a Styrofoam-like texture. But, at least with the Norwegian grandmas, I was getting attention and touch. "You sweet little China doll," one said, and they all stroked my hair adoringly.

China had dominated my childhood view of Asian Americanness in all manner of ways—from bucktoothed Bugs Bunny doing yellowface and the "fa ra ra ra ra"–singing waiters serving duck to Ralphie's family in *A Christmas Story* to Wayne heavy metal yelling Cantonese to woo Tia Carrere in *Wayne's World*. Silly. Servicing. Sometimes sexy. But still silly? When mistaken for Chinese or when she thought I risked being subsumed under the pan-Chinese umbrella in America while "mmm" inhaling orange chicken, my mother reminded me of the history behind the hierarchy. "For one THOUSAND years," she said as she morphed into the jaw-jutting posture of a revolutionary's statue, "China tried to take over Việt Nam. But they never can. Why? Hmm? Why?"

"Because we're better?"

"In Hô Xuân Hương, there is a turtle," and I'd settle in as she launched into the legend of Lê Lợi.

Feeling testy one day, I asked, "Didn't bà ngoại say she is part Chinese?"

My mom pursed her lips. "Your grandma is a lot of things," she replied, widening her eyes. "Everyone thinks they're Chinese. Don't start me on Bruce Lee. For one THOUSAND years . . ."

I knew I wasn't Chinese.

However, I let myself be their China doll. Maybe it was the marzipan or being called "kjære." It was an early, but definitely not the only, memory of acquiescing to the pull of pan-Asianness. Just so that I could belong to something, even if by mistake.

Firklover wrappers
Crinkle in bunad pockets.
Marzipan pig waits.

CHAPTER 2

Three decades later, the Sons of Norway helped me recognize Edvard Munch's name in an empty gallery of an art museum in Portland, Oregon, where women's skin bore no stories of the sun. In his *Young Girl in a Landscape*, the unnamed is jaundiced and featureless, her arms and legs fading into the yellowing background. Munch neglected her. She lacked lips, teeth, tongue, so her call came from deeper. Fill and finish me, she pleaded.

I stared at her, ignored in her tiny eight-by-eleven frame, from beneath plucked and drawn brows that still disappeared in sunlight that I had harnessed into darkening and lightening my skin that I had treated and abused and healed. The Norse grannies had lost me but also helped me find the marks of a young yellowed girl who blended into a landscape, yearning but not showing that she wanted to be found.

PHOTO ALBUM 1

Fixed by salt, John Adamson's mid-nineteenth-century print, *An Athlete*, depicts a lean, muscular, barrel-chested man, heavy in beard and serious in brow, in shorts and Roman sandals. His fists clenched, he leans his weight onto his left leg, the other extended behind him as if he is lunging or running into battle. This is, the J. Paul Getty collection handbook states, "the first person ever to be photographed in a way that expresses animation rather than the static immobility that the slow process of early photography required. We are not seeing actual motion that has been arrested, but rather a cleverly staged illusion."

The immutable salt—the "I love you" mineral—fixes the illusion of forward movement as a reality, a truth. All I can taste is salt as I piece together photos of the woman moving toward the time she became my mother and then away from me. But there wasn't a before and after. It was both—toward and away, then and now—in each one of the photographs of my mother:

> Someone's camera
> In Việt Nam caught my mother
> at thirteen, posed and

PHOTO ALBUM 1

Cautious to not waste stillness
Before the permanent wind.

First family pic:
"Cute," she says about me, to
Her, "Long time ago."

She unbends the crease, laughs at
My dad, "Tennessee racist!"

In a rare candid
Aunts and cousins make faces
While mom cradles me

Smiling, yet Polaroid flash
Illuminates her regret.

Her boyfriends closed doors
Her Nikon clicked "sexy shows."
Viet ballads wail mood.

Crumpled in trash: her robe slips
Less sexy than my dolls fuck.

Museum of her,
Her house curates her beauty
Pre- and post-nose jobs.

In her room, only wedding
Photos of her all alone.

My mother turned the camera on me too. Desperately, critically, sometimes for hours, re-posing my elbow, poking my hips and shoulders to suck in my bulging child belly, asking what was wrong with my face when it moped from exhaustion of staring at my mother's face obscured by the telescoping lens. For every one out of twenty negatives, she'd approve with "dễ thương," which translates to "easy to love."

In Italo Calvino's "The Adventure of a Photographer," the narrator warns, "The minute you start saying something, 'Ah, how beautiful! We must photograph it!' you are already close to the view of the person who thinks that everything that is not photographed is lost, as if it had never existed, and that therefore, in order really to live, you must photograph as much as you can, and to photograph as much as you can you must either live in the most photographable way possible, or else consider photographable every moment of your life. The first course leads to stupidity; the second to madness."

She forced light, my face.
Outfitted, posed my body.
Shadows slimmed my nose.

Face hidden behind the lens
She twists, zooms, chasing ideals.

First school picture day,
She curls my hair, pulls on pink
Dress and white stockings.

Weeks later, she throws photos—
Crooked smile, a blink—
that scratch.

Two against the world
One photo captured candid:
She chased and I blurred.

Another: on the toilet
Stuck and embarrassed, but seen.

After nine, "Not cute,"
Photographs stopped,
catching me
Only in the margins.

Relieved about my absence
Until my girls ask to see.

When we are grown, my sister captures our mother peeling white grapefruit skin in a detached flower, plump teardrops of pulp clinging to her still delicate jasmine-soft hands, though her knuckles are gnarled from rheumatoid arthritis. "No milk in Việt Nam," she explains. Her long thumbnail digs into the crown of the fruit and pushes down until her thumb sinks entirely between the skin and meat of the grapefruit. I reach for the salt and begin sprinkling on a citrus wedge. "In Việt Nam," she begins, as she does with so many stories, "my brothers used to stuff their shirts with grapefruits and rub up against me to get more space in our bed." My sister and I exchange a quick glance, slightly creeped, but she laughs, and we know to never interrupt that. "Five of us in one bed. And fake boobs pushed me to the edge."

PHOTO ALBUM 1

She places the flower of grapefruit skin upside down on her head, like a bonnet. My sister pulls out her phone-camera. Like a reflex, my mother shows urgency and waves me into the picture. I make a goofy face, pushing my lips out, flaring my nostrils, and rolling my eyes. It was a way for me to exaggerate the nose she taught me to see as too big, the chin she told me was too weak, and the eyes she reminded me were sunken like my dad's, "like zombie."

When my sister shows me the photo on her screen, my monkeyface looks ridiculous next to my mother's. In the moment of my sister's click, her teeth-baring laugh had reverted to the same controlled smile, sleepy eyes—just like that picture of her at thirteen—except, this time, the grapefruit pulp shines between her ugly-beautiful fingers. There is movement of life in its glossy wetness, its squeeze before the audible pop, its travel from her hands to our mouths.

My mother clicks her tongue at the face I've made in the picture. It cannot be contained by any wood or glass, on any wall, in my mother's photographic history of herself.

CHAPTER 3

GHOST STORIES

In the handful of years I had before I started ripping my hair out, I lived in a haunted house that made the hairs on my neck and arms stand on end as if from an electric touch. The housing project was my residence of record, but I spent a lot of time at my grandparents' house just a few miles up in the lower hills of Pedro. Whereas most people associate their grandparents' home with comfort and cookies, mine had me grasping for control in a constant state of threat and danger. It felt as though I was living in the foreboding world of the film *Poltergeist* that traumatized me when I was far too young to be watching it. But nobody noticed how scared I was. I don't want to do that to you. Instead, I want to spin the story so that, at Halloween time, ghosts are comforting reminders that not everything ends, nothing ever completely dies. Ghosts are merely protectors whose spirits persist. And you are strong enough to protect yourself, to survive.

In a family from Việt Nam, I was always-already surrounded by ghosts. My mom told me all about the ghosts wandering our homeland where, it makes sense, millions of people dying from thousands of years of foreign invasions would linger and mourn. In their Saigon apartment, a little girl floated in the bathroom and then unfurled a long, pointy tongue that made my girl-mother pass out. In the same place, a force had pinned the pressure

CHAPTER 3

point on my grandmother's palms to the bed. The scariest part of these stories was the threat that we wouldn't even be able to rest when we're dead. My mother, though, reminded me that we weren't in Việt Nam anymore so I wouldn't know a real ghost even if I saw one.

Yet, when she told me these stories, I goosebumped. My stomach dropped. My shoulders weighed heavy. It felt true in my body that ghosts carried and followed. It seemed impossible to escape their shadow. I feared that I was not strong enough to stand on my own against something that could possess me, so, when I felt the goosebumping, I turned on the TV so that the voices kept me company and in safety. Often left by myself in my grandparents' house, I watched a VHS of *E. T.: The Extra-Terrestrial* on loop, frantically pushing the rewind button when it ended to seek comfort in a kid who found himself in a friend with a blinding heart longing for home.

While these inherited ghost stories made me vulnerable and perpetually in danger, sensing these spectres' presence also made me feel special, powered. If only I knew either of my languages well enough to concoct an alchemy of words, I could make you understand how the ghosts thickened the air of my grandparents' house to seep into and stay with me. Like a telekinetic, I would make your hairs dance. If I could, then people wouldn't incessantly ask me what is wrong. They would just *feel* it the way I did.

Instead, I'll try to give you a tour, as our people are often expected to do. This tour, though, is different because it serves *us*. Tours are powerful because they can be validating. This place is here. This happened here. Even if I sound crazy, you might get goosebumps. Our bodies remember that this was, is, true.

This is a place I return to often. This is the entry hall. Take off your shoes. My grandfather doesn't; he wears his Dickies carpenter jumpsuit and work boots all day. The shoes track dirt into the house, and the black tiles in the entryway showcase all the grime from the outside world. I don't understand who would choose pizza box–sized slabs of black granite for the entryway to a home. The dirt bothers me more every day, even after my bà ngoại sweeps with her bong co broom. It's like an itch I can't scratch.

This is also where my grandfather pressed the blow-dryer to my hair so closely that it burned white. I could smell my hair dying, but I silenced myself. He'd been in the military for decades. The only way he knew how to care was rough. And if my facial expression so much as hinted at a complaint, I would be shut down with stories about his shitting in front of AWOL Nazis in the German forest or how bad the people had it in Africa, where he also served. So, I watched my newly dead hairs float down to lie like scratch marks on the black tile. I loved him.

The living room is here on the right. There's lots of unused stuff in here. The piano is just a shelf for pictures; the black and white ones are from Việt Nam. We only eat at that dining room table on Thanksgiving, so I mostly just hide under it to sneak my bà ngoại's Sucrets lozenges. This room is where my family yelled and threw things at each other. Actually, that's every room. Don't look at the crack across the ceiling for too long because it'll start to look like it is widening.

This happened when I broke my arm. My bà ngoại was babysitting a pigtailed blonde toddler from down the street but stepped out to buy cigarettes or gamble at the casino. I'm not sure how much time passed. The little girl was in a playpen and started crying for milk, so I climbed up on a plastic chair made for squatting briefly to inhale Saigon street food. I was just able to reach high enough to drop the bottle over the edge of the playpen when the chair cracked beneath me and a force pushed me flat to the floor, knocking the wind out of me. I was immobilized long enough for the kid to drink her bottle, fall asleep, then wake up and gaze at me still lying there. Though my body was frozen, I could roll my head from side to side enough to see that I was only inches from the big stone hearth of the fireplace. I stared at the ceiling, cracked like the bones in my right arm. A stranger was courting my mother in Honolulu, so I lay waiting for my grandmother for what felt like hours. When she came back and saw me flat on the floor, she cried, "What you do?"

Since my bà ngoại could not read street signs and couldn't drive anywhere outside of her memorized paths to the casino or friends' houses, my teenaged cô drove me to the hospital. (And, yes, "cô" designates paternal aunties, but I never called my mom's one sister the "dì" for maternal aunties. Our family didn't exactly follow the rules.)

CHAPTER 3

The ER waiting room at County literally bled into the hallways. I was placed in a room with a young man who moaned through the night. The only company I had were doctors that came in to do, what I realize now, were examinations to determine if I was being physically or sexually abused. They told me to watch wind-up animal toys circling and jumping on my meal tray while they inspected my vagina and rectum. I returned to my grandparents' house with a cast and sling, and my dad came to visit with Disney books and a Pee-wee Herman doll to comfort me.

We're gonna go back to the entryway where a hallway branches off to the other half of the house. I'm going to give you a warning that I never received. When we enter the hallway, it'll feel like someone is following you too closely behind your right shoulder. Then the weight will press you down until you want to scream but you're too heavy to make space for your voice to release. Just keep walking. Stay close to me. I'll protect you. I'll talk to you about anything and everything, just to remind it that we are alive. We'll hum '60s girl group bops. Our energies will make each other stronger against it.

On your right is my bà ngoại's bedroom. The windows are foiled over so it's always dark and she can drift in and out of Việt Nam time. Enough light shines through the seams between different sheets of aluminum foil to illuminate the stranger's silhouette lying in her bed. Sometimes, Bà Ngoại said, it would lie beside her and look at her, eyes shimmering.

Let's duck into the bedroom on the left to lighten the hallway weight. I have some good memories in this room so those will keep us safer. This is where I admired my cô's '80s cool—the Aquanetted hair and heavy-lidded liner that every night brought boys pebbling the window. When she answered the pebbles and snuck out, I would snuggle in her empty bed, sniffing her lingering perfume and listening to her Duran Duran and Depeche Mode records that lulled me to sleep. This is when the closet lights would flick on and off, and sheets snaked and knotted around my ankles so I couldn't stand when I woke from being pushed off the bed. The little girl who'd died in that room didn't want to see that I was growing taller than her, that she'd never become the teenager my auntie was, slipping out the window into the wild night. One time when my cô did stay in bed with me we snuggled in the middle of the bed and told funny stories and fart jokes. It was fun. I felt loved.

Until I was rolled out of my auntie's arms and off the bed. I lay on the floor, looking up at Cô leaning over the edge. "Why did you do that? Get up here, silly."

Years later, my cô's room became my cousin's. As a baby, he stared and cooed at the closet whose light would turn on and off during my married-in aunt's late-night feedings. It was the same closet where I'd spent hours hiding-playing, organizing odds and ends into extra shoeboxes. Just as my father had his collections, my grandmother and mother saved and saved in a desperate remembering and filling what was lost or what never was. In their shadow, I packed my own boxes with everything kỷ niệm, from a purple Crayola that smelled the perfect balance between wax and paper to a Chinatown satin coin purse that, when rubbed against my lips, made my legs want to kick and run to a ceramic E.T. bank that my mom had surprised me with one day after work. I don't think she realized that I obsessively stroked the grooves on E.T.'s skin to soothe his lonely displacement and longing that strummed a chord deep inside. Kỷ niệm.

That's what scared me. I spent all that time in the closet with *it*. I unknowingly let it see the things that meant the most to me, the things that I would carry with me in shoeboxes to every house I would ever live in. It saw me. What would it do with that knowing?

When he grew into a talking toddler, my cousin told his mother about the monster in the closet and drew pictures of devilish figures contorting and raging and killing.

Your skin is crawling, so let's cross the hall to the bedroom I shared with my mom. The built-in bookcases were my favorite part of the whole house, and I wanted to fill them with more than just the encyclopedias my grandfather ordered on layaway and the crystal animal figures my mom brought me from Ports O' Call. I'm sure my mother was lying to me when she said that our things toppled off the shelves because the house was built on a fault line. I know it wasn't tectonic friction that sent corners of books plunging into my face at night. When it became my uncle and his wife's room, they would hear their own voices karaoked, calling to each other. "It felt," my married-in aunt told me, "like it was trying to get into me, through your uncle." Then, one night, she watched a frost grow over the

CHAPTER 3

sliding glass door that opened up to the backyard trees heavy with fruit at the end of summer.

There's one more room. It was a haphazard addition, constructed as a human-sized shoebox with revolving purposes.

In the '80s, that room belonged to my youngest uncle, who once opened his closet to show me his guns, proud of the semiautomatic he posed with in a firing position to teach me the grammar of guns. When pigeons cooed and swung on the telephone lines hanging across my grandparents' backyard, my uncle popped the screen off his window. One of his rifles peeked its muzzle out, sweeping, raising, spraying. Feathers. The telephone wire swung up like the jump rope in the Double Dutch sessions I watched at school but was never good enough to join.

The army had disrupted what would have been a father-son legacy. Whereas my grandfather had survived multiple wars, my uncle went to a school where kids bullied him for his gook middle name and chinky eyes. They blamed him for their dads coming back fucked up, so they berated and beat my uncle for reminding them.

All the birds could have been reincarnated spirits. Shot out of the sky, they could have been looking for another body. I didn't feel strong enough to resist such an intrusion, so I began to worry that the ghosts would follow or inhabit me and I would be haunted forever. Maybe they were why I seemed hell-bent on destroying myself, including trying to suffocate myself with a pillow at five years old but pretending I was hugging it when my mom walked into the falling books room. Was there a type of ghost that amused itself by trying to get a little girl to kill herself just to escape her fears? Was there a type of ghost so committed that, even as an adult, the same hair-raising fear followed me when I looked out the window, dreading going outside to the noise, movement, and faces of the world? What would it be like to live a life without always thinking about dying?

In the post-embargo '90s, this room housed my eldest uncle and his wife and children, all of whom were denominated "Illegal Alien" on little laminated cards. I was so excited to have cousins to play with, to not be alone in this house often for hours on end, that I stayed and slept in this room, selfishly blind to the fact that I was adding a fifth body to the cramped space.

One night, while lying on my back in their shared bed, my stomach erupted. Vomit sprayed up and then fountained down into my eyes, my hair, and all over their bed. "Cay mắt quá," I cried and rubbed my eyes, the chunks sticking in between my fingers. Unable to see clearly, I crawled across the thick green carpet to my uncle who was stationed as he was every night, sitting by the window with the glowing cherry of a cigarette stub that he sucked on between nose picks and loogie grunt-rattles. Calm, he wiped my eyes with the hem of his t-shirt until I could see well enough to run to the bathroom and rinse the bile clumping in my lashes.

Though I've suffered nausea, constipation, and general GI distress all my life, I've also always been afflicted by a wonder whether my body was not possessed by some sort of poltergeist, haunted by the spirits of this house, or the ghosts that were made in that green-carpeted shoebox. As an adult, I watched *Paranormal Activity* and was convinced it was a documentary of how an angry ghost from Việt Nam, or from my grandfather's military tours across the world, possessed me with a very particular mission: to make me pull my hair. Each pluck some paranormal prank. This is why I stopped watching scary movies.

There was only one room in my grandparents' house where I didn't feel afraid.

The bathroom was light blue from the wallpaper to the toilet seat where my grandfather had wheezed his last breaths and Bing Crosby impressions. ("White Christmas," I learned later from books, crooned from the same speakers that blasted the air raid sirens, the ones that propelled my mom and uncles, running with skyward glances, to check for the twist and scream of napalm canisters.) I'd heard that my aunt's friend had gone to use the bathroom in the middle of the night only to find his outline sitting and smoking. On his porcelain throne, he burned the rest of the ghosts away. Even after multiple visits from exorcizing priests, the house didn't lighten until my grandfather passed and did his final tour of protecting us.

When my aunt told me this my skin goosebumped and my eyes welled up and spilled over. I wish I'd been the one to see him. I was so desperate that the last time I ever saw him would not be as he was cremated (I was the only child in the family witnessing), his lips glossed pink in the

CHAPTER 3

embalmer's piss-poor attempt to manufacture some last vestige of life in that made-to-be-burned cardboard box. I was only ten, but I was not fooled. My longing was clear: I wanted to feel chosen, to feel that my grandpa was still there to keep me living.

CHAPTER 4

THE WHITE NBA

From the tumult of fear and danger, I clung to the control and order of my father's closet. It was packed, hangers tight with t-shirts that catalog his life—games, concerts, conventions. On the closet floor, fishing tackle boxes of halved index cards with all the zip codes in Orange County, California, which he memorized for his job as a parcel sorter. Behind those, binders of coins and stamps—histories of the world curated through pocket scraps—and stacks of long card boxes marked by his careful handwriting: *Topps, '56–'58; Angels, '89–'94; Dinosaurs Attack!*

My dad was meticulous. Every other weekend, we played Mouse Trap and Guess Who? until we graduated to points-based games like Monopoly, Scattergories, and Scrabble—winners all accounted for in my dad's tightly handwritten columns. Even on our most special out-of-routine visits to Disneyland, he estimated the carnival-equivalent cost of each ride based on duration and fun in order to multiply that figure by the number of rides we could get on from gates' open to close. "Are we getting our money's worth?" my dad asked in line as he checked his stopwatch. Our fun was calculated. Because my dad had epilepsy, I was committed to bringing him more joy than stress, to maximize our fun numbers.

CHAPTER 4

During my weekends with him, he took me to card conventions. With me gripping my copy of his handwritten checklist, we followed his systematic snaking through each aisle, our fingertips scented with the plasticity of the card sheets flipping, flipping, flipping. I unfolded the checklist on which my dad's handwriting was starting to blur from my sweaty palms. But at the top of the list, I could still read clearly: *NBA, White Guys*. There were rookie cards for familiar names like Larry Bird and Vlade Divac, and a lot of other unchecked boxes next to names that sounded like they were characters in my Sweet Valley Kids books.

"Because they're the minority, the underdog," he'd told me in the car. The vehicle smelled of rubber bands stacked around his gearshift from his graveyard shift sorting parcels. "They're shorter, not as strong, but they play right alongside the Black guys that are better than them. And they still win."

In his justification, I heard echoes of what my Vietnamese mother said about my dad and all other white men. In the tides of their words, I struggled for footing, thumbing through pages of Black NBA player cards, whose noses often looked more like mine than John Stockton's did. The rare Chinese player was, of course, seen as a foreign freak: Asian *and* tall?

But what my dad showed me about the need, the drive, to check off boxes, to complete a set, was intoxicating, exhaustingly pleasing. I followed through on this elusive mission. I pulled a Little Twin Stars marker from my Hello Kitty purse—hallmarks of Asian American girlhood—and checked off boxes on my dad's list. "Look! Mark Eaton!"

"Local guy. Good find."

"She's so excited," the card seller said to my dad. "Who's your assistant collector?"

"My daughter," my dad replied.

"Huh," he said, unconvinced, and handed back our change and a plastic sleeve for our white NBA players. (Later, in my adolescence, convention exhibitors would regularly assume that I was my dad's wife—an unexpected and unnerving effect of being the mixed-up product of a white dad and Vietnamese mom.)

My dad did not express guilt or discomfort but tried to make up for it. He showed his love through collectibles. The hard stick of gum from the

Garbage Pail Kids pack left white powder on my fingers, and I licked it off as my jaw tired from chewing. Nasty Nancy. Tattoo Lou. Oozy Suzy.

When we got back to his house, we spread out our findings on the floor. My dad ran his thumb across the glossy photos and flipped to the cardboard backs to mumble stats and facts about each player. His mind was cataloging all of what we'd found together, and I helped him slip each find into its plastic bed and click the sheets into the binder rings. Satisfaction.

By the end of the night, my brain, eyes, and jaw were tired. I leaned my head on the coffee table where, earlier, my dad and I had finished one of our many puzzles together. This one was of Disney's Snow White. He taught me to build the border first. "Straight edges line up like this," he showed me. "Always build the frame first." The pieces were cool against my cheek, and I ran my palm over the seams of pieces and the gloss of the glue. Order. Stability.

The next morning, always a heavy Sunday, my dad dropped me off at the curb in front of my mom's apartment, my backpack a little heavier with the stack of duplicate cards. It was not easy to hide things from her, but I tucked one of each card inside my books—the one place she never looked. I couldn't let her know that I was collecting too. When she'd split from my dad, she dumped binders of his baseball cards into the bathtub full of water. Some she took a razor blade to, slashing the players' squinting faces and destroying the neat, even rows of statistics. Every once in a while, at the card conventions, my dad sighed when he came across a pristine copy of a baseball card that my mother had ruined.

Angry and victorious, she'd retold this revenge story to me many times. "Stupid game," she always said. "Big men chase little ball. Play game all day. So stupid!" I would nod because disagreeing would restart the whole retelling. Due in part to poverty and in part to my mother's resentment of American privilege, I was never allowed to play organized team sports, and the "no" was always expressed through criticism of my entitlement, frivolousness, and selfishness—all things I would hear when pulling my hair or cutting myself in the after-school hours when my body could have been at practice.

My dad always seemed disappointed I did not become an athlete, shaking his head and muttering, "If only you had lived with me . . ." My body—sedentary save for the atoms vibrating and colliding until my buzzing hands picked, plucked, and ripped—was a constant reminder to both of my parents of what they did not have.

"And your dad," she'd say, getting angrier at what was clearly disappointment on my face, "so much time. So much money." She looked as if she were going to cry here. I wished that I could have known her as a child and that she'd let me hold her and tell her she was meant to live. "To collect," she'd say. "Collect what?!"

Here was my mother, mourning a childhood without games, without collections. Here was my father, careful in curating the past he loved and that he wanted to share as a gesture of his love for me. Here was I between them, growing with a need to collect and organize things that didn't make sense, that hurt. I would lose myself many times in checking off boxes of lists of things that weren't me—a collection always remaking itself.

CHAPTER 5

MS. ONO

My compulsion to organize and sort and, ultimately, control anything and everything mushroomed at school. The papers in my desk and Lisa Frank folder were filed by date, size, and color—in that order—and my Hello Kitty pencil case, complete with button-activated drawers, was the epitome of mechanized efficiency, like the map of a fabled city. In this case organized to compensate for the mercuriality of moods at home, the pencils' engineering was being tested by my growing anxiety and obsessive compulsions, which school was reinforcing and rewarding.

The beast showed out too much, though, when Ms. Ono began to teach us cursive writing. I was wearing out the enamel on my pencils and calluses were hardening on my fingers. When I wrote, I pressed so hard that I ripped my ditto sheets. This made me spiral into guilt for ruining something that Ms. Ono then had to reprimand and replace. My physical inability to let go or loosen up wasn't just about the loops and the uppercase "Q" that just doesn't make any sense. My grip was holding on to something deeper.

Ms. Ono's long black braid swung across her back as her feet shuffled across our fourth-grade classroom. I longed for hair so thick that I could full-hand grip it. Even pre-pulling, my strands of hair were thin and

CHAPTER 5

wispy, like spiderwebs carried off on the wind. Her thick hair made me want to chew.

On Culture Day, Ms. Ono pinned plumeria in her hair and told us about the Big Island. The kids pulled their eyes into slits and cried "O-no!" I didn't say anything. Regretted that I never did. But I wanted to protect her, just as she did me. She was the one who saw me unbraiding, unmoored by all the things school showed me I didn't know and the way I clung to her.

Ms. Ono called my mother for a special conference. My mom begrudgingly accepted. She was already not just wary, but downright resentful, of everything I learned and everyone I met at school. It embarrassed her whenever I made a mistake, and it saddened-angered her when I did well. As a result, I perfected the art of flying under the radar, which was easier than it seemed in an educational system that attempted to tame children to sit still and stay quiet. But Ms. Ono was the only teacher who picked up on inklings of what was brewing underneath my stillness and silence. Being seen by her caused me to start slipping.

Since I suffered from insomnia and night terrors as a child, I often struggled to wake up in the morning. One such morning, my mom was rushing me out the door to school with a half-eaten Svenhard's Danish wrapped in a paper towel. As I slung my backpack on one shoulder, I realized the zipper was in the exact same spot as it was when I left school the day before. I had forgotten to do my homework. It was uncharacteristic of me, always taking care of homework and all forms requiring a parent signature—all the little things so that she wouldn't have to. I was afraid to admit it, but she knew by the way I froze at the threshold of our apartment door. "I'll write a note about why you late," she sighed.

My paralysis electrified into a frenzy as I pressed my spelling words worksheet against the back of the door and squeezed my pencil to perfect the curves and lines of each mimicked letter, every invented sentence. It wasn't that there was pressure to fulfill the myth of the "model minority," which we clearly weren't, but rather an expectation to lie or perform just to not disprove it. When my mom returned with a note folded with the origami precision of one of the quainter Asian stereotypes, I was already on the fourth out of the five required sentences. "Whoa, con ơi," she marveled.

"So fast. The last word . . ." She'd always been proud to teach me words in English. She once distinguished "sympathy" and "empathy" to me, stressing how important it was to never sympathize. She was ready to help me: "How about—"

Before she could offer her suggestion, I jotted down a sentence that defined the spelling word through context. Even some of my letters were sloppy because I was in such a rush to prove to her that I didn't need her help, that I wouldn't be a problem. I proudly packed up my homework and looked to her for approval. But her "wow" sounded more sad than anything else. She brushed past me. "Go," she said, undoing the three locks on our door. The wrath born from grieving for what she did not have wreaked a special havoc on me. This was what the straight-A student, model minority myth didn't account for: I was the trigger of my mother's worst insecurities and regrets. Everything I did caused my mother to relive all that she'd suffered and all that she'd never had.

Once the conference date arrived, I was unnerved to have my mother and Ms. Ono together in the same room. Aside from the one time I glimpsed her tuft of '80s perm briefly appear at the auditorium door during one of my district-wide spelling bees, my mother didn't typically go to the school; often it was the Latchkey aide Stephanie in her cool Members Only jackets who dropped me off in the mornings in her revving Mustang, and my grandfather picked me up (sometimes one or three hours late) in his sputtering brown El Camino. To have my mother on campus, let alone with Ms. Ono in the same room, was like witnessing some kind of scientific demonstration. Push-pull. Ice-fire.

My mother smiled and nodded at Ms. Ono's suggestions about how to relax me—exercises, arts and crafts, reassurances and all things that would never happen. I would continue to play countless games of the Solitaire my dad had taught me and subject my Barbies to fatal natural disasters.

Ms. Ono asked me to sit at my desk and write my name. As I did, she pointed out to my mother how my fingers squeezed calluses into their tips and the rigidity of my wrist created a pressure that would steadily hurt my body and my writing. "Mmm," my mother nodded, arms crossed. She wanted the monopoly on stating what was wrong with me. "Okay, thank you, Mrs. Uno."

CHAPTER 5

"It's Ono," my teacher replied in her Asian autopilot pronunciation-correcting voice. Then, a slight tonal shift indicated she realized that my mother was trying to put her in her place: "And it's Ms."

"Mmmhmm." My mother pursed her lips with a self-righteousness that I didn't understand, given that the closest she was to married was resolving child support disputes with my dad while rotating a carousel of suitors. But she was an expert in making others feel bad for simply being who they were.

Back in the car, my mom complained that my teacher was too nosy, her lipstick too bright. She took me to Pic 'n' Save to buy rubber pencil grips to cushion my calluses. This was the extent of the resolution—a ninety-nine cent gesture to cover up wounds that just needed time and attention.

We never talked about my pencil problem again. I learned to keep school things silent.

The Rickey Henderson baseball card that the boy I loved (and who later died) gifted me, I kept in my school desk.

At Christmastime, Ms. Ono invited me and my quiet friend Juana—also a firstborn daughter to immigrants—to her home to bake cookies. I had never made Christmas cookies before. I didn't realize that you could. I just thought that these were things you bought at the white people's non-durian grocery stores. "Christmas?" my mom huffed indignantly when I made the mistake of asking about her childhood across the Pacific. "How poor people buy presents tầm bậy tầm bạ?" She scoffed. "No fat Santa."

In Ms. Ono's home, I learned that she slipped her shoes off at the door. Like me. She put sugar on avocados. Like me. She salted watermelon. Like me. *And* she celebrated Christmas, all warm and fat and gifted.

In my time with her, I felt that she saw me more than my mother could. Ms. Ono gifted me a sense of belonging in a system that otherwise felt like it would go on with or without me. She noticed me clinging and gave me a chance to let go. Though I still can't fully release my grip, I am grateful that she saw me and tried to teach my hand another way.

CHAPTER 6

DEAR RIDER STRONG

Dear Rider,

    I always finished my homework early and alone, because my mother didn't feel that she knew enough English to help, so that I could watch you on *Boy Meets World*. Your gap-toothed mischievous grin, your chokers, your hair-flipping. Your hair was so thick.

I did not feel about you the way I did about Lou Diamond Phillips portraying Ritchie Valens or Leon Robinson as a saint in Madonna's music video for "Like a Prayer." Yet, you occupied me.

The boys who were labeled bad at my school were black or brown, but we didn't have any like you. You were a white bad boy, which is a good bad

CHAPTER 6

boy. And you made being wounded look so cool. I thought you would understand and that you would then elevate me to your level, turn my hurt into cool too.

So I took risks for you. There had just been another shooting in our housing project when I asked my mom if I could walk to the store by myself. I think she only said yes because it was just a domestic dispute, which is not a term in the Vietnamese language that I grew up with. Because outside was dangerous, I was both scared and excited to venture out on my own.

I followed her advice to walk like I knew where I was going, as if I was up to urgent business, even if I felt scared or got lost. No eye contact. That invites people to kidnap you, she'd warned. I passed the landlord's office where I'd perform my mother's slanted stories to get extended grace periods on the rent check. I passed the laundromat where I played boat in the rolling carts and collected empty boxes of single-use dryer sheets to make beds for my toys that I took extra good care of so as not to seem ungrateful to her passing glares.

I hurried past the TCBY frozen yogurt shop where my mom and I met my dad when he picked me up on his weekends; she didn't want him coming to our door anymore. Her new boyfriend was jealous and resentful that my dad was white. Like you. Maybe she would be jealous of you, too.

I made it to the Lucky's supermarket that greeted me with the swish of automated doors and a gust of air conditioning. I felt fancy. Maybe that was why I didn't stoop to steal you on the cover of *Tiger Beat* magazine. Maybe it was because my mom told me that when she, at the same age I was when I fell in love with you, tried to steal an apple from the market but was interrupted by Việt Cộng spraying bullets. One killed her neighbor who dropped dead in front of her where she hid in a drainage ditch. I can still hear the thud. As kids do, she thought that everything bad that happened was because of her. So did I. I paid for the *Tiger Beat* with money I'd found or saved from lost teeth.

I paid, but I still felt ashamed. She'd always taught me not to flush my pee in order to save money on the water bill, and here I was spending money on magazines. I slipped it under my shirt and into my outgrown waistband as I walked up the stairs to our unit. She zeroed in on my paper-flat stomach immediately. I hurried to the bedroom she and I shared, and for some reason she let me go.

When she was home, I'd sit in the closet where I usually pretended that my dolls faced catastrophic forces of nature, barely surviving. Here, I organized toys so that I appeared to be doing something while I daydreamed of you, whom I protected from the worst of my imagination. Daydreaming was a risk too, a waste of time, I'd been told. When she was gone, I pulled the magazine out from under our mattress or in between the volumes of books my dad sent me—anywhere I thought she wouldn't look and find you, this desire I had outside of her. I stared at your pictures until my vision blurred you into movement—winking, beckoning—whatever I thought romantic gestures were at ten years old.

When the pages were worn enough for me to start flipping through the rest of the magazine, I discovered addresses in the back. There were PO boxes of agencies where readers—I—could write letters to teen heartthrobs—you, the good bad white boy.

I wrote you a letter. It started out normal enough. I mimicked niceties about your show. *You're a really good actor.* Then I conflated you and your

CHAPTER 6

character. *I feel bad that your dad isn't around.* Then it got sad fast. I wrote to you about how stressful it was to be poor and not have enough money to help my mom out because she was always stressed and that's why a part of me didn't want to help her, which makes me feel guilty, and then she brings these boyfriends over—I miss my dad as much as you, or Shawn, did on the show—because I know she hopes they will pay some of our bills, but that means more time my mom spends away from me, and that is good and bad. Even though we can't understand each other, we're all the other has.

I held onto the letter for days. I was afraid to send it because then you'd know me—you'd know her—better than anybody. I didn't tell anyone anything. I didn't think anything I had to say was important, but here I was putting it all in rainbow Bic ink and getting all congested from tearing up but holding it in.

When she found the magazine, Mom said she always wanted a kid who was famous. "The world will always need entertainers," she'd told me.

So I decided to send the letter. My dad worked at the post office, so I always had holiday stamps. I mailed a Christmas stamp to you in the summer.

It wasn't until fall that you responded. I tied my hair up in a high ponytail—"palm tree," my mom called it—so that it wouldn't distract me as I read your response. My hands trembled as I sliced open the envelope imprinted with more postal ink than you'd think it would take to get a letter from the nice part of LA to our part of LA. There was a lot of possibility in that moment.

I'd hoped that you'd read every word and grow a crush on me and make me famous too, not because I was suffering, but because of how I wrote about it, how I was surviving it.

You responded with merely a signed photograph.

I knew it was fake too. My mom had shown me how to tell the difference when I had to sign some documents for her. You'd had some assistant open my letter, unfold my life in ink, and stamp your signature on a black-and-white picture of you perched on the type of stool that I imagine they have in acting classes. You treated me the same as everyone else who wrote you a letter. I sat in the closet with my hurt and the photograph, barely surviving.

I told my dad when I wrote the letter—not what was in it—but just that I had. I told him I used one of the stamps he gave me. He said it was cool, and I remember feeling better about it, then. My dad, after all, was the one who showed me movies and shows and music and taught me to love all of it. But something in me must have known that parental "cool" was just to cover up concern about this kid's new phase of writing fat letters to strangers. I must have known, at some level, that no one thought what I was doing was "cool," certainly not you. I must have known because I burned your generic response with a match from my mom's fishbowl collection of matchbooks from restaurants her boyfriends took her to.

I'm writing this to you now so that we both remember what I created and what we destroyed. You probably won't read this one either. But at least I'll know that I said it. At least I'll know that, even after something dies, it can grow again.

CHAPTER 7

THÚY

My mother had decided she would marry one of the boyfriends in her rotation because, I could tell, she was tired of being poor and alone with me. She lay on her stomach, her beautiful face propped in her hands, and her legs waving behind her nervously, like the young, carefree teenage girl she never got to be. I sat on the floor beside the bed that we shared.

"Which one should I marry?" she asked. I thought about these men who were now, for the first time, my choices. One of them scared me. Another got mad at my mother for laughing when I threw up on the leather interior of his backseat. One was nice but chemicals from the war, seeped into the soil that fed him, rendered him impotent. Another lived in Seattle. The only other option I remembered was a man who had a face like a plate and was equally as silent, save for a tasteless pussy joke he had told my mother in Vietnamese while I was in the room, as if I couldn't understand because I looked more like my Irish Norwegian father. This boyfriend had a steady job and wanted to have children.

So, at ten years old, I thought that I was giving my mother the gift of a life of ease. "Him," I said.

Their marriage felt quick, my soon-to-be brother's feet pressing against my mother's taut belly skin—and then he was born with a full head of

CHAPTER 7

dark hair. With the outline of this new family shape darkening, the managers of the housing development in which my mother and I had lived for years—alone, together—was no longer accepting the tear-filled stories that my mother rehearsed with me and then pushed me out the door to deliver. Leaving before she got kicked out of the projects for sneaking in her new baby daddy with a job, my mother moved us to Orange County—away from my school, my grandparents, aunties and uncles.

In my mother's rush, we did not have a new home to go to, so we moved into a room at my new stepfather's parents' house. Like each of his five siblings and their families, we shared one room, the four of us sleeping on two mattresses pushed together. Although this intergenerational familial living is common to many Asian families, mine hadn't exactly been traditional. We were fragmented. And I had gotten used to my mother and I confronting the world alone.

Now I had a corner. There, I was allowed my miniature boombox and an Ace of Base CD (before I learned that it was a soundtrack for white supremacy) and an Oingo Boingo tape (before I learned Danny Elfman was sexually harassing in between composing), as well as a blank cassette for recording songs off the radio, a small box of plastic jewelry, Polly Pockets, *Wizard of Oz* trading cards, and a portfolio of fictitious families that I used to draw. Little things.

My mother's husband's family whispered about me being white, not knowing—or maybe knowing—that I understood their Vietnamese words. One of the sisters—the "crazy" one with bad acne—sat cross-legged with me in my corner to listen to my boombox. "They call you Mr. Personality because you so ugly," we sang along with Gillette. Aside from this, I was hungry for school to start and open up a space for me beyond that house that was in no way a home.

The school smelled different. The kids were white and well-dressed. Apparently, across county lines, overalls became cool. The morning bell was a long beep instead of a shrill ring. I was seated across from a tall, pale student named Olaf whose Norwegian name gave me hope of familiarity. I had seen kids like him at Sons of Norway holiday parties where I was fawned over as the "China doll." Olaf's eyes moved down to my advanced breasts and wiggled his eyebrows and said, "Welcome, new girl. Let me know if you need anything," to which his deskmate responded with a low-five. Wordlessly, I shifted in my seat to shoulder my shirt to hang over my chest. I'd always been jealous of how men hit on my mom everywhere we went, but this made me feel the way I did when the random guy from the Cabrillo Marina (and some others) elevated to stalker status.

I looked at a ditto sheet in front of me, the lines and letters bleeding purple from bad copy. I stared at it, squinted, thinking that at some point my eyes would come to focus on a clean line and some sort of order would appear. I squinted again, trying to see. It was in this squinting that my own eyelashes came into view. My mother had always said that in addition to wanting to chop three inches from my giraffe legs and add them to hers, she coveted my eyelashes—long, thick, dark, and curled up at the tip. With my eye muscles twitching in concentration, I could bring these long dark fibers into sharp focus and they cut across the white and messy purple ink of the ditto sheet. Black cutting across white. I imagined catching an eyelash between my index finger and thumb, plucking it from my eyelid and laying it across the clean, white page.

Of course, I did none of this. Over the previous couple of months in the house-not-a-home, trapped in a room with a newborn baby brother (and another sibling on the way) capturing all the attention of my increasingly distant, resentful mother, I had learned not to draw attention to myself. My way of coping with childhood—from minor cuts and bruises to more permanent scars of disappointment, fear, and instability—was shaped by not wanting to burden my mother with problems. I filled in the ditto feverishly, my legs restless, almost aching, through the rest of the school day in anticipation of pulling that black eyelash and setting it against white.

During class as I was trying to avoid Olaf's glances and smirks, a woman called me out and led me to a picnic bench on a grassy median that ran between two classrooms. I wondered if I was in trouble. The classroom windows were one-way, so all I could see on their black glassy exterior was my own reflection staring back at me, wondering if my new schoolmates on the other side would be witnessing some kind of punishment. The woman

CHAPTER 7

said nothing to me before she pulled from a folder a laminated card with a black ink drawing of a bird on it. She leaned across the table toward me.

"Can you," she said slowly, pausing here, as if she would have added the Vietnamese equivalent if she knew that language at all, "tell. Me. What. This. Is?" That's when I understood that my mother had filled in "Vietnamese" under "Language Spoken at Home" on the Emergency Information Card when she had registered me for school. I had listened to people talk to my mother this way, as if she were stupid instead of bilingual.

"Yes," I said. "That. Is. A. Bird," emphasizing that "errr" that my family says they hear in their heads when they think of English.

"Oh," she responded, shuffling the rest of the cards back into the folder. She checked off something on a form and sent me back to class.

At recess, girls huddled and whispered about a boy named Huy. He looked like my cousins—all high cheekbones and crooked teeth and sagging Levi's, but the girls swooned, and the boys thought he was cool because he pronounced "that" like "dat," these Orange County kids thinking it was a hip-hop thing, like Q-Tip in Tribe's "Award Tour."

I said, "Hi, Huy," my lips flexed into the gentle push of the soft Vietnamese "h," like my grandmother who renamed herself after the fallen ancient capital, followed by the half smile of "uy" like gliding down a slide.

"It's Hoy," he said, correcting my pronunciation. "Like 'today.' Spanish."

"It's okay," I said. I swallowed a choking sensation. "I'm Vietnamese too. I can say it right."

"Look, I don't need your fob shit wrecking my game. Make yourself useful and ask Jackie if she likes me."

I walked away. *Fob?* I was so used to being dismissed by Vietnamese people for being "too white" and patronized by whites for looking "too ethnic." But never a "fob."

I saw Jackie, the cute Mexican girl that Huy—sorry, *Hoy*—was pretending not to notice, as she expectantly watched me approach, and I redirected my path to an empty tetherball court. Later, he saw me in a flat-footed squat over a banner our class was painting for the square dance.

"Hey," he said. "Saigon squat." I looked up at him. He looked at me. And that was the last time we spoke.

On the walk to the house I measured my steps carefully so as not to step on any cracks or to place either one of my feet to pavement an unequal number of times. And since I had no one to walk with, I murmured "The Sign" lyrics: "No one's gonna drag you up to get into the light where you belong..." (Insert here a retroactive shudder at the now obviously neo-Nazi lyrics.) I tapped my fingers against my thighs as if they were typing the letters I uttered.

Back when it was just me and her, my mother regularly asked me to tweeze her gray hairs. I was always excited for this because it meant we would have time together. Sometimes I told her I was still looking for gray hairs, even though I knew I had gotten them all, so that I could spend more time with her. This ritual was itself an echo of the past. When my mother was a little girl, her grandmother asked my mother to pull the gray hairs from her head, always in the morning. My great-grandmother sat on a stool as my mother stood above her, twirling each waist-length gray hair around her finger and tugging it until the scalp broke. My mother said she always placed each hair on my great-grandmother's lap, so that she could see them against her black pants.

"Weren't there a lot of hairs to pull when she got old?" I asked my mother during one of the many times she recounted this story of Việt Nam to me. "Did she expect you to pluck her head bald?"

My mother responded, "No, by the time her husband died, she shaved off all of her long hair and never let it grow back again."

Around the same time in Việt Nam, my mother was getting her hairs pulled as well. One of her older brothers was making money off of cricket fights with men and boys in the neighborhood. Before every fight, he jumped on my mother and held her down to pull her long, thick, dark hairs to jostle the cricket's antennae so they were agitated when the fight began. My mother hated this. When she tells this story now, she clicks her tongue at my uncle as if he is still alive.

"He is such a mean guy," she said. He is my namesake in Vietnamese.

Then she began to weed me out. My mother asked her rotation of boyfriends, then her baby daddy, to tweeze not only her gray hairs but also her underarm hair and leg hair. This ritual, behind a door ajar that I peered

CHAPTER 7

through, fostered a strain of jealousy. *They* got to pull those hairs, parts of my mother's body, and once they were pulled, they were no longer part of her. Bearing witness seeded in me the promise that pulling my hair was a way to get back to her.

In that crowded house, I retreated to the invisibility of my corner to pull my first eyelash. It was thick and black. Its root was wet and pulpy, and I could feel a rim of moisture around the follicle in my eyelid from which it had been plucked. I dragged it, moist and plump, against my lower lip the way I did with my satin-lined baby blanket. The fragile threshold between my interior body and the outside air became crystalline sharp. Every lash I plucked thereafter teetered me on the edge of that boundary.

My mother uprooted me twice. When I complained about this second move, my mother offered no sympathy. Sorry, empathy. She had been displaced across an ocean and then shuttled between multiple cities, so our moves were inconsequential to her, if not a reason for my gratitude. When my baby sister was born red-cheeked and gentle, we moved again to have more space and to where I would have my own room. The school in this new neighborhood was full of kids who looked older, as if they bought their own clothes and went out on dates. Kids played soccer as part of an organization and with moms who brought them single-serving snacks during practice and didn't ride the bus and got new clothes every school year and kids with homemade lunches outnumbered the kids with lunch tickets.

The most popular boy in school was in my class. His name was Brett Smith, but his blonde, teenage-bodied girlfriend called him by his middle name, Scott, and everyone seemed to see that as very grown up and distinguished. I arrested my eyeroll. Unlike LA, popularity was not achieved by how many fights you'd won or how quickly you could shit-talk. At this new school, it was all Scott's slick-backed hair and name-brand clothes.

On my first day of a new sixth grade, I wore a Limited Too shirt: burgundy, with an American flag. With her husband's paychecks, my mother, who must have been feeling the pressure too, bought me two brand-name shirts: Limited Too and Gap. "Rotate," she said and tied my hair up high in my favorite "palm tree" style.

This was my chance. When the teacher introduced me, kids who looked so much older than twelve swiveled their well-gelled and combed heads, their better brand-name shirts swishing as they turned. Their looks were brief, unimpressed, and they whispered to Brett. He didn't look at me immediately, and in that moment I thought that maybe my life would change, that I would no longer be the mixed transplanted diaspora girl from the projects but be remade as the new queen of a school where people would bring me little bags of Doritos and tiny bottles of Gatorade. But after a few beats he glanced my way and, with equal disappointment and disgust, muttered, "That's her?"

The only one who talked to me was a girl named Jennifer who had also recently moved there. From Oklahoma.

These Orange County kids scoffed at all the things I didn't know: Ancient empires. Phylum, genus, species. Dividing decimals. Extracurricular sports. Allowances. Lip gloss. Packed lunches. The boys made fun of my hairy legs, and at snack time girls offered me their crackers and gummies that later I found out they had licked or rolled on the carpet. I kept my head down hoping no one noticed I was lost, responded minimally to the Oklahoman, and waited in line silently for my turn at their handball court, learning their new rules.

Then, I wasn't the newest kid anymore. Thúy.

Into our classroom, her face rose round like the moon, reddening when her overbite, yellow, smiled for her. I could tell she, too, had dressed up for her first day of class at this new school. The kids snickered at what was clearly her father's best Cosby-style sweater, woven and knitted all different colors, hanging from her narrow shoulders over her black pajama pants—the same that my grandma wore to go out to the casino. Her clothes had absorbed the scents of eucalyptus oil and incense, of temple and markets. Even though she smelled like home to me, she dwarfed my stupid, small struggle. She wracked me with guilt. I wanted to grasp her cheeks and press my face into hers until her jaw jutted into my palms, first in a smile at my touch, and then in anger.

The teacher instructed us to say her name as the pronoun "we" with a "t" at the beginning. We all said her name in unison and many giggled. The

CHAPTER 7

class was not able to pronounce the accent to her name, letting the sweet, light sound fall flat. Hers was the same name of the girl in the Vietnamese children's books I had read growing up. I could say that Thúy went to the library, the supermarket, the playground with her friends. I knew just the words. In Thúy, I was confronting my own stories.

I shifted in my seat. I wanted to look away, but I couldn't help staring at Thúy's frightened eyes darting back and forth in her moon face, pockmarked and grinning and bowing to every question that the teacher asked her, turning and smiling to every classmate that laughed at her inability to respond.

"Thúy is from Vietnam," I heard Mrs. Hale say. "She doesn't know much English, so we will have to help her out. Jade," she said. I looked up, startled. "I said, could you please translate for Thúy? Your file says that Vietnamese is the language you speak at home." All of the Orange County kids looked at me, surprised to learn what I'd been trying to hide between my alternating brand-name shirts. I nodded and silently cursed my mother for writing "Vietnamese spoken at home" on the Emergency Information Card again. Then I remembered that she didn't speak Vietnamese to me much anymore, mostly to my siblings, and she hadn't filled out the Emergency Information Card for me this time anyway. I had. I had checked that box because I wanted to reassert myself as Vietnamese, as hers.

"Well, you can help translate for Thúy." Mrs. Hale turned to Thúy and began gesturing at the air between us. "Thúy. Jade. Vietnamese."

When I didn't move or respond, the teacher repeated, "Jade." Now they were giggling at me.

"Um, okay," I mumbled.

Thúy responded, "I. Like. America."

The kids snickered around the room. Thúy smiled at me, and in her face, I saw the high cheekbones and worried eyes of all the women in my family staring back at me, pleading for help in the only way I could help them.

I confess that I packed up my stuff and hurried out of the room before Thúy could. I paired up with other kids, even if they rolled their eyes. I squeezed in at the end of the lunch table so she couldn't sit next to me.

I avoided her by laughing harder at all the other kids' dumb sex jokes, by initiating conversations about lip gloss with girls I hated, by leaving our native tongue in silence.

She snuck up on me in the handball line.

"Chi, ơi," she made me so uncomfortable calling me *older sister*. The familiarity, the respect, the tenderness.

"Do you like it here?" she asked.

I scanned the handball and basketball courts, the tetherball lines, the monkey bars to see if anyone noticed her talking to me. I shrugged, "Không sao."

"Wow, you speak so fluently for being so American," she said, excited. This is the one thing I knew better than anyone else in the class. At least until Thúy came.

"So why do these American kids look so much older?" She nudged my elbow. "Is that boy nice?"

"He's as dumb as he is cute," I told her. She giggled and clutched my arm the way my mother did when we were sharing a joke in Vietnamese in a crowd of English speakers.

I caught myself smiling at Thúy when the Oklahoman trotted up behind us in line. "What're y'all talking about?"

I wriggled out of Thúy's grip and told her I was explaining the rules of handball.

Out of the corner of my eye, I could see Thúy's head drop. The girl started chatting her up and braiding Thúy's long dark hair, as they both giggled.

I turned my back to them and took my turn hitting.

So we remained strangers, a dual-edged displacement.

I set a record number of absences. "So sick," I groaned to my mother, of course in Vietnamese.

Bouncing her new baby, in her *real* family, she waved the absence notes I wrote aside, so I signed them for her and lay in bed reading under the blankets, blinking away Thúy's face peering back at me through the English words.

CHAPTER 7

During my absences, I plucked. I became acutely aware of how each individual lash had a hot, wet pulp of a root seeded in the layer of self between my skin and my insides. I began to choose which hairs to pluck based on their differences in coarseness, color, length, and if the ends were split. But by the time my eyelids were barren, I had realized that difference was subjective. Every lash was different in its own way and that was reason enough for me to pull it. This made me focus on my body out of interest rather than the usual self-consciousness and shame. As a child expected to be an adult and one who was constantly listening to stories of Việt Nam, I felt time folding in on itself and accordioning back out. Pulling my hair allowed me to focus on one moment in the present and forget about other timelines. Time slowed and ballooned, so much so that I could spend hours tugging and targeting choice plucks without realizing how much daylight had passed.

The rim of my eyelids and the patches of dwindling lashes became positive and negative spaces, the lashes still wet rooted under my skin and the bald spots dry without the lashes to protect them from sun, wind, and my fingers. I watched myself tug my quickly thinning lashes, holding my eyes open dry and focused to catch the exact moment when the root broke the skin and the lash became no longer my body but an external thing, disposable. For many lashes, blood pooled from the follicle in a little bubble of red, and my eyelids grew puffy for a day or two afterward.

The lashless eye is unsettling, like a lizard's, dimensionless like a fresco painting. The shadow cast by lashes under Southern California sunshine is easy to take for granted until it's gone. In its place, an uncanny valley where I didn't look like a complete human but only because I was overwhelmed by amplified human feelings that led me to pluck and then to worry about the glaring flatness of my eyes.

In her own brand of love, my mother threatened to beat my hands with chopsticks to help me stop. "I used to do that," she said. "Then I just stopped. Easy."

I couldn't stop but I committed to finding ways to harness the behavior myself. I wore mittens or taped my fingers together at night when my brain kept me up long after everyone else was asleep. I drew pictures of what my eyes looked like with sparse lashes, trying to disgust myself out of the habit. I even used a cotton swab to brush water on my eyelids in an effort to soothe the areas inflamed from plucking. Then I tried milk because my mother and every other Viet auntie always credited the American drink for why I was already so much taller than them. When I felt the urge to pluck, I ripped strips of paper or popped bubble wrap or pulled grapes from their stems. None of these substitutions replicated the simultaneously satisfying and unsettling pain of taking something from my body and making it not of my body.

Plucking was exhausting. Resisting the urge to pluck was even more exhausting. But I could not fully rest.

I dreamed differently. My body opened up and transformed—a thorn in my thumb became a tentacle with which I attacked small children, my toenails ripped off and the meat underneath became purple oatmeal, and I picked at, widened, and eventually fell into cavernous pores in my face. It was no coincidence that I usually woke up from these dreams to find my hands in the phantom movements of plucking, scratching at my eyes so hard that I often uprooted my remaining lashes. I found them scattered across my cheeks in the morning. Changed, I awoke like the octopus that could morph color, texture, and shape all while dreaming.

When I returned to class, no one seemed to notice. I was relieved that no one heckled my lizard eyes. I held my eyes level, staring into the distance, so my lids' baldness could not be seen as easily.

The popular girls in class now orbited around her, braiding, giggling, helping Thúy, who could now say to me in English, "What's up?" She played handball, lunging at the ball so hard that when she missed, her braid swung around her and slapped her in the face. She laughed along with everyone.

I sat down next to the Oklahoman whom Thúy had already left behind. "Teacher Ma'am told us you were having family problems. You okay?"

I looked at Thúy who was smiling at me from across the room. Ashamed, I responded, "That's right."

The school year ended shortly after I returned from my long absence, and we were all funneled into different middle schools. But Thúy is still with me, in regret, in hope. I think of her often. I dream of her. I see Thúy on the handball court, her braid swinging, twirling.

CHAPTER 8

PUPPETEER

When I entered the middle school counselor's office, my English class journal was on her desk. Sticky notes flagged pages of "concern." I'd become bad at school math, even though numbers eclipsed most of my thoughts: how many steps I'd taken, how many letters were in each word I said, whether the number of hairs I'd pulled that day was even or odd (it had to end on even), and how symmetrical the hesitant slits on my wrist were. I pulled my sleeves down over the self-inflicted cuts on my forearm and stared straight at her to minimize the visibility of my bald eyelids—a stupid but never-ending performance to hide what's not even there. Without needing to look, I picked at the freckle on my right knee, comforted by the slow scratch erosion of my marked skin as I waited for another woman to punish me for what I had said.

I can't remember what I had written in my journal. I don't remember exactly what she asked me. I can't remember exactly what I told her.

What I do remember is that she—the counselor assigned to mental health concerns—began to cry. "That is just so sad," she sniffed through tears. It was disorienting. My feelings had always been dismissed as trivial in comparison to my mother's epic suffering, but now this lady was crying for me? Attention? Worry? Pity? This new dynamic gave me a manic surge of energy.

CHAPTER 8

So I dug in. "... and he leaves the room whenever I come in ... and she writes me letters because no one wanted me to be born anyway ... and two boys asked me out as a joke this year ... another boy actually had a crush on me but then found out I was Vietnamese and did the 'heil, Hitler' salute and never talked to me again, but I'm like I get that you're a white supremacist but how bad is your eyesi—yes, it's a true story ... and another true story is that my uncle, well—here's another tissue ..."

When I returned to class, I sat down next to a classmate who'd also been sent to the counselor for something he'd written in his journal. "What happened?" I asked, eager to commiserate.

"Nothing," he said. "I told her everything was fine, and she let me go."

That had never crossed my mind. I wondered why and what that said about me. "Oh," I said.

Jennifer and I walked home with two baggy-jeaned Adams who were in a separate social circle while school was in session. We all laughed so hard that I forgot, for a little bit, about the counselor.

The crying counselor placed me in Dramatic Arts.

She tried to do something right. She could tell I was used to being invisible and needed to be seen. She picked up on my fantasizing and longing to make myself much bigger than what I was plucking and cutting away. She couldn't have known, but maybe felt, that I come from a line of women who can dance their way into new countries, who can put everyone else's mẹ to shame during the karaoke renditions of "Unchained Melody" and "Careless Whisper" at Vietnamese weddings. Maybe I could channel all that I had learned from my mother about putting up a front. Maybe this class was my first step to becoming the famous actress or singer my mother hoped for. Maybe this class would get me closer to Rider Strong. I had the hope that movies and plays promised. But I wouldn't show it.

The teacher's stomach entered first, as pregnant as her bowl cut was boyish in the way it spun on her ever-shaking head, feather-dusting her perma-furrowed brows. Her eyes were glossy like licked hard candy, and they poured on the first day of class.

"He left me alone," she said, and filled bell-to-bell with the story of how her husband cheated on her with a man—men—contracted AIDS, died, and left her alone with their two children and one on the way. Sobs shook her shoulders and belly, flanked by framed posters of famous musicals, jaws frozen open in song. The few boys in class pretended to shove dick-shaped things into the poster people's agape mouths.

Up until that point, all I'd seen of what I'd been told was gay were the men dressed like women in *Paris by Night* comedy sketches, my mother's laugh hissing at their batting lashes, rouged cheeks, and dick jokes. She never said the word, only pantomimed the comedians' swaying hips, limp wrists, and coy kisses to air. I had only just been introduced to Rickie on *My So-Called Life* who represented a gay teen as a full human, but I was honestly too engrossed in Jordan Catalano.

It would be years before my cousins taught our elders the power of transitioned pronouns and loving vows whispered between women. I would never be so brave in our culture, so there was no need to tell me to be silent about this.

Each of our teacher's revelations was punctuated by the belly-to-bowl shaking stomp of her chunk-heeled loafer. "Oh shit," she said post-stomp. "I pissed myself."

The boy sitting in front of me dropped his head between his knees so that he was just a round hump. The tension in the air harnessed me from tracing the symmetrical crescent of his back with my restless finger. She returned a few minutes later to the room of eyes sherlocking for drip stains.

The teacher made us audition. Her well of mourning thunked the piano keys as I shuffled forward, and her boiled sweet-glossy eyes beamed blue at me until I mimicked her mouth 'O' and tried to match the key tones. "I can't hear you," she yelled, shaking her blonde bowl. Two languages choked me, but I pushed sound. She shifted her hands down the ivory body and thumped the keys harder, faster. "Your voice is supposed to change," she yelled. I could see her hands punishing, her lips tightening, her brow sweating, as her body, pregnant with the life of a death, heaved music into the piano between us.

But, for the life of me, I couldn't hear the fucking difference. "Match the music," she hollered. Everyone was watching now, and I could feel those in the audition line behind me telepath, "Don't fuck this up for us. Don't

CHAPTER 8

push her over the edge." Desperate, I Ricola-yodeled at the top of my lungs, hoping that some rise or dip would meet its sonic match from her chapped and lonely fingertips. "For fuck's sake!" and she was off to the back dressing room where we could hear her filling tissues.

I was assigned to the puppet chorus, all of me hidden by a sheet except for the felt puppet with my hand shoved inside, burning with the widening and tightening of fingers as mouth—the pain of being background player to the purple-eyeshadowed girl cast as lead, the one who hugged the teacher and brought her unborn heather-lined gifts.

One day, our teacher wasn't there. In her place was a bald man with long hair who wore black and gesticulated as if always in soliloquy.

He was not a musicals guy, and that made me want to thank the baby Jesus. The first exercise this sub gave us was a dinner party as characters from *Beetlejuice*. This is it, I thought. My dad had showed me all of his favorite films revolving around death, from B-movie horror flicks like *Blood Feast* to classic adaptations like *Stand by Me*. And, of course, the whole Tim Burton catalogue. The other kids didn't know *Beetlejuice* like I did—from the sway of Geena Davis's floral dress to Juno's emphysema rattle and Otho in his flamboyant séance. This is when drama would become me, when I could finally be believed as another.

For the first time, I spoke in class, volunteering to be Lydia. I'd pined over Winona Ryder in *Mermaids*, *Heathers*, and, the crush-maker, *Edward Scissorhands*—all peroxide blonde and dancing in scissored snow. She'd introduced me to the yearning for wrists more delicate than mine, to feel things for which I didn't know words.

Thrumming with excitement on "action!" I mimicked teenaged Winona Ryder's sallow-eyed slouch, and before it was my turn to speak, my heart pushed out of my throat the words, "It's all so fucking terrible."

I looked to the sub for validation. His bald scalp sheened in the light and for a moment I wondered if—hoped that—he was a hair puller like me. He tilted into a Robert De Niro impression, right corner of his mouth fishhooking back, "You talkin' to us?" *He* got the applause, and I switched back to silent.

Our teacher returned at the end of the semester to direct the Christmas play with a flatter stomach and a new ring on her finger. She told us about a decades-long friend, also a piano player, whom she met in *Into the Woods*. "My baby has a father now," she told us, and I popped my wrists.

I signed up for a second semester of drama because, even though I was a tone-deaf terrible student, I was curious. When she called my name in roll call, disappointment shadowed the gloss of her eyes when she heard my monotone, "Here." That night, I replayed the disappointment, disdain, hatred that clouded her face at my mere presence, and I pulled a bushel of eyelashes, the ones at the corners that really hurt and made my eyes water.

In this new semester, Valentine's Day grams shuffled to and from hands around me, new lists of most fuckable girls got gummed to the bathroom walls, my boobs got bigger so my shirts hung baggier.

I puppeteered the *shit* out of the green felt–faced farmer who smelled like the sweaty palms of other beaten-down drama students before me, probably the ones who suffered her wrath during her husband's illness—the weight loss, the sores, the skin sensitive to anyone who did or did not want to touch. I puppeteered until my hands cramped and my forearms ached and burned. As painful as it was to be this desperate to please, to make up for what hadn't been for this recklessly weeping and yelling mother who just wanted me to sing, I found solace in exhausting myself until I did not have the energy to pluck any more lashes. It was a relief to feel pain somewhere other than my puffed, raw eyelids.

Even though I was clearly not cut out to be a movie star, I had to keep working harder, to fill time with something, anything, that kept me from being alone with my self-hating hands. My drama teacher taught me that no one would find me, let alone make me the star of any show, if I wasn't willing to do more than puppet.

INTERLUDE-INTRUSION

Tug tug tug tug tug tug tug tugtug tugtugtug tugtugtugtug

Pop

Puuuullll

Pop

Pull pop pull pluck pop

sssshhhh

CHAPTER 9

PERIOD

While I was still in junior high school, my mom started taking hairstylist classes at the local community center. She had me sit in a little plastic chair while she shuffled around me in a Saigon squat, clipping, separating, spraying, and trimming my hair with her fancy new industry scissors. "Trán dô," she muttered at my bangs, but with a side smile. Because there was no act of love without criticism.

My mother worked double time. As she cut my hair, she acted as the gatekeeper of Vietnamese culture and identity. Oftentimes this worked by criticizing what I was doing as "not Vietnamese," instructing me on how to be "more Vietnamese," and then, when I tried it, pointing out how I was failing at something I was born into. I was taught to think of myself as a failure just by being myself, that aperture of "Vietnameseness" shrinking me out of the frame.

"In Việt Nam, it's bad luck to tell the kid they're beautiful or smart. They would grow up thinking that's true and then become the opposite. Ugly. Stupid."

"We Vietnamese don't smile like you Americans just grinning walking down the street. People will think you're creepy or want something."

"We don't hug. It's just not our culture."

CHAPTER 9

I accepted it all because the tingle of my mother's fingers in my hair was worth it, but the "we," the "you," the "the kid" were all linguistic pinches that sunk into dull aches, the feeling that the sound "cô đơn" makes from deep in my chest. I was raised to be lonely. Even from myself.

Maybe it was because I really was the cứng đầu American kid who relentlessly frustrated my mother that I kept seeking ways to tunnel through the loneliness masoned around me. I tried to hug her and was pushed away with a "Where did you learn that from? I didn't teach you that." It is with my hard head that I believe when I was young enough to not remember, my mother hugged me. I have seen pictures of her holding me as an infant, tender and unalone. But the only instance that I can remember her initiating hugging me is when, at twelve years old, I emerged from the bathroom with a sigh and confessed, "I started my period. Can I have a pad?"

I had learned early on not to ask for anything so as not risk the impossible dumptrucking of guilt that usually began with "In Việt Nam, I had nothing . . ." I taught myself to do everything myself, from filling out school forms and doing homework to playing alone in my imagination and consoling myself during insomnia and nightmares. So when I did have to resort to asking for her help, I was matter-of-fact and short. This would minimize the chances of her getting mad while I was talking and reduce the number of microexpressions—lips tightening, eyes narrowing into full "bitch, please" side-eye liếc, back of wrist brushing her flyaways—that I would exhaust myself trying to decipher and brace against.

I was completely unprepared for her to go in for the hug. I was used to bad touches, or, at least, avoidance of touch. I stood there in rictus, arms stiff at my sides, as she held me. At this age, I was already a head taller than her, so her face lay uncomfortably against my chest. "You're a woman now. You'll feel so much better when it all comes out. You'll be clean." Clean. I already struggled so much with the feeling of being unclean. Being poor. Being Vietnamese. Being Mỹ lai. When my monthly cycle aligned with a full moon, I was now subject to Confucian principles of cleanliness too. At temple, Mẹ put a hand to my legs to stop me from shuffling off my shoes to enter and pray. "Có kinh," she told me. "Đừng dô." So I stayed outside just getting whiffs of incense planted in dry rice to lift people's prayers and secrets aloft.

Since that first day that I plucked an eyelash, I have prayed for the strength to stop doing this to myself, to stop ruining my face and making everyone around me uncomfortable about what is missing. I have prayed for Phật Bà to protect me from whatever trailing poltergeist might be possessing me to do this to myself, despite every daily resistance.

My prayers didn't make it. I had not been able to go more than a few days without pulling an eyelash. One of my goth friends from school came over one day—a rare occasion that my mom allowed an outsider into her house—and became frustrated that the heavy dark eyeliner she was applying to my lids kept smearing because I didn't have lashes to hold the color. "Just let them grow out," she said. "You'd look so much better." She said it as if it was so easy, as if I had any measure of control over it. I scrubbed the top of a 7 Up can before handing it to her. "See?!" she said, laughing but annoyed. "You've got problems."

In later years, therapists would tell me that I should focus on the time that I am making it without pulling, even if for an hour, and recognize that as progress and possibility. Yet I couldn't help but see it as a loss.

Though hairpulling continues to be a daily punishment of myself and a grieving for what I could have looked like and who I could have been if not for thinking about and doing this every day and night, waking and sleeping, the urge is always strongest the week before my period. Every month I am bleeding and more hairless. I wish I were a fun PMS bitch that people make memes about. Sweatpants and chocolate? Get it, girl! A hot pad and a glass of white wine? It's five o'clock somewhere, honey!

Instead, I am incessantly visualizing my eyelids sparse and coarse as the evening silhouettes of desert trees. I am erasing the eyes, flipping those lids inside out, microscoping in like the Magic School Bus to machete away the bramble of nerves, subcutaneous tissue, and floating pulpy glands in my eyelids. I face the roots of those remaining lashes from the inside. I touch the wet bulb nestled in its follicular membrane, and this juicy nest makes my thighs tingle. I grip the vessels and feel the blood pulsing to the root to nurse the lash for what is meant to be its two-month life but will be much shorter in my hand.

The glorious intricacy of the anatomy of one of the most fleeting of body parts is matched only by what feels like a primal thrust to destroy it. To rip

CHAPTER 9

it from me. To find every hair that is different and uproot it, only to realize that every single one of them is different. To clean the slate. To remake my eyelids, designed to protect me, and render them bare. Swollen and bleeding. To scratch out all that bound me stiff in my mother's embrace.

CHAPTER 10

THERAPIST 1

The crying counselor referred me to a psychologist. The shame lived in all my mother's sighs and slaps on the steering wheel during the drive to his office, and later in every lash I pulled to physicalize the unstoppable guilt. Therapy was seen not only as white but as weak for asking for help for privileged "problems" and, even more so, a betrayal of the culture and our family. My mother warned me about falling into traps of history, of letting white people in, let alone telling us what to do or blatantly lying. Again. "Don't tell him what year I came here," she warned. "Don't tell him how much money your stepfather makes. Don't tell him anything stupid that will make police come to my door again."

"Yes, got it, Mom."

"Don't tell him—"

She waited in the parking lot with big sunglasses and a wide-brimmed hat on, even though she stayed in the car. Leave it to my Vietnamese mother to disassociate from me in the most Hollywood style.

This first therapist wore cowboy boots. He didn't look at me, just asked questions and checked off a list. He sent me to the psychiatrist next door. There were prescriptions and weeks of increasing dosages. And then he undid any progress I might have been making when he forgot who I was while I was right in front of him.

CHAPTER 10

I was poring over Hollywood tabloids in the waiting room when he emerged yelling, inflection and tumbling consonants like aural turaco birds: "Get out! You-ah crazy, huh? Never-ah come back-ah!"

His patient pulled his hood over his face and stormed past, his wind flipping my magazine pages. "Fuuuuck you, sadist!"

"Burn it!" He tossed the patient's file on the receptionist's desk. "Next," he huffed as he looked at the next file and then to me.

"So sorry," he said.

"No problem," I assured him. My upbringing kept me calm during fits of rage and violence but made me spiral from the slightest twinges in someone's brow.

I sat down in his office and, as usual, covered myself with a throw pillow. He fumbled apologies with each shake of his head. He must have been feeling like a walking stereotype. If I were him, I'd have been afraid to be the gesticulating Italian, shouting from behind the pizza counter. What could it be like to have all this power and still be mocked with impressions of that little pixelated plumber? He was a "wahoo!" launching out of a sewer pipe to save a princess whose hair is shaped like her dress.

But he was a doctor. He prescribed pills that changed people's brain chemistry. He did mine. He approved a bottle of antidepressants that made me hallucinate during history class and while doing my chores. When I disobeyed all instruction and went cold turkey, I hallucinated that my dead grandfather was surveilling me through a glass orb, and I dreamed that his angry ghost filled my bedroom with flashing light and explosive noise until I was cast out of my own room and what felt like out of his love. I did not tell the doctor any of this.

He clicked his pen against his clipboarded checklist. He stared at me. The birds outside the window were quiet.

I said, "I'm sorry?"

"I say, how is the Valium we added, Jennifer?"

"No Valium," I said. "And my name isn't Jennifer. It's Jade, Lexapro."

He studied his clipboard, then jumped up from his armchair, muttering in Italian.

I was grateful that he switched to a language I didn't understand. It made me feel better about being the thing that happened after the worst part of his day. I never returned.

INTERLUDE-INTRUSION

Brush brusssshhhh brusssssshhhh

Pinch

T
w i
s
t

Rip

Yes yes yes yes

Skin rippling. Inner thighs aching. Knees touch.
Pick me Pick Pick Pick

INTERLUDE-INTRUSION

Yank Rip Yank Rip Yank Rip Yank Rip

N
o
N
o
N
o

Rub Rub Rub

CHAPTER 11

THERAPIST 2

This insurance-approved therapist looked like New York. An ankle-length black coat—a duster, I'd read once in a book, maybe a duster—draped in such a way to allow the peek of class. Not classiness as I knew it in Vietnamese contexts. This therapist did not showcase Louis Vuitton or Chanel logos. This was white people, old money kind of classy, like a modern art museum or a political cartoon: a crisp high white collar, a long string of artsy large black and gold beads, and knee-high leather boots that looked made for a power strut down a Manhattan sidewalk. Her smooth gray hair was accordingly attuned to shape and form, and her chunky framed glasses made all of her facial features look dainty, which tortured my insecurities.

My mother's clothespins hadn't tamed my nose that bulged into my line of sight until all I could see was the sheen of oil pooling in my gaping pores. I always caught people looking at my "trán" fivehead that my hair was now too thin to cover with bangs. That grief weighed down my way-past-baby-fat cheeks and deepened my Resting Bitch Face perma-pout that always provoked people to ask, "What's wrong?" or "Why are you upset?" As if in response, my chin melted cowardly into my neck so that my mother regularly patted it upwards with the back of her hand. "Double chin no good," she affirmed as her chin taps clicked my teeth together.

CHAPTER 11

"Even though you're sad, you're so beautiful now," the therapist said. I could not process how fucked up this bullshit was to say to a girl my age going through what I was going through. Because when she leaned forward and repeated, "You're beautiful," I felt this surge of excitement that maybe I was. Maybe, despite all of my sadness-induced coma-like states and incessant thoughts of hurting myself into oblivion, I was beautiful. The educated, cosmopolitan fashionista of a therapist (basically a doctor of the mind, the center of the universe) said so. I was beautiful. Therapy worked.

However, as she leaned back into her chair, she reached for her steaming tea and said, "I can't imagine how gorgeous you'd be if you were happy." Now I had to work toward being beautiful. I didn't even know what was wrong with me, let alone solutions for crawling out of sad-pretty to happy-pretty. Beauty seemed impossible with the nose, chin (or lack thereof), teeth, and skin I had been trained to hate, to pick at and angle to strive toward acceptable, but never pretty. It felt as though she was mocking me by presenting this impossible project. She was laughing at me.

This therapist was dead to me.

It wasn't until decades later that I learned complex trauma survivors often react in extreme measure to the seemingly most minuscule facial expression or comment.

Luckily, a knock at her office door interrupted my trying to summon what I still believed to be latent telekinesis to smack her big fat glasses off. With a swish of her duster, she rose to open the door, and in walked a clone of her from thirty years ago. Same boots, same coat, same accessories, same angular face. The only difference was her hair hadn't grayed yet. It was black and stringy. "This is my daughter," she said and welcomed her into our session as if it were an open teatime to ponder philosophies of aesthetics. I wondered what would possess a person to duplicate their parent to such costume precision. While I was running away, grasping for anything that would fit me, here was a grown woman choosing to run toward her mother.

"This is Jade," the therapist told her daughter who was handing back a set of keys. "Isn't she beautiful?" A momentary dart of the daughter's eyes said everything before she said, "Mm hm, yeah." Nausea surged through me.

"I've got to go now," I lied. "I hear my mom honking from the parking lot."

The therapist's brows knitted but I walked out before she could question or protest. As I exited through the lobby, I could hear mother and daughter debating which kind of salad to order for lunch. I never returned to her.

CHAPTER 12

TROLL

It started with prayer.

I shadowed my mother around the temple through incense smoke and whispers to ancestors. That's what the monk who'd read my mother's palms when she was nineteen years old called me—her shadow. He'd mapped out everything from my father's stooped shoulders to my sister's skin color to my mother's eventual death. There I was, in those creases and chains, following.

At Phật Bà's porcelain and gold feet, we kneeled and shook the fortune sticks out of the cup to the insistent rhythm of our hopes, and the color-coded fortunes laid out whole what I was to be for the year. I prayed for good numbers so that my mother wouldn't be resigned to agree that I was just a người xấu số, the unlucky numbers that all the depression and anxiety and hairpulling could be chalked up to. It was all about the numbers. I was dividing.

My mother had once told me that the hour of my birth imbued me with the spirit of water, but not just any dribbling faucet or rain-reliant stream. No, I was the ocean. "People might shit in you or be scared of you," she said, "but they can't live without you." Maybe this was a way for her to express her love to me. I yearned for the power of this promise. I could not feel it.

CHAPTER 12

She read, too, that my lucky color was black, so I began to wear it everywhere, even at temple where the rainbow of áo dai fluttered in the breeze of the temple gardens.

I longed for closeness but kept distance from my mother as she walked the grounds, pausing to bow to each of the Buddha statues seated under trees, above fountains. She only pulled me close by the elbow when we came to the grapefruit tree, my height to harvest.

Though never completely comfortable with her at the temple, it was what we had of closeness and peace. And the other option hadn't offered any of that. At one of my uncle's weddings, the church was big and velvety, and a Christ hung before us and the flesh grayed next to the bleeding gashes on his emaciated stomach. Hungry for distraction, I reached for the book in front of me, but let it splay on my lap when I could not follow hymns and psalms in Vietnamese, Latin, and an English I did not recognize. The trilingual ceremony stretched on; I caught words about "man and wife" to "serve" and "obey" and kept my mother in the corner of my eye to mimic when she stood and knelt and did the sign of the cross. (The French had built memories into her Buddhist body.) When each pew rose to follow my uncle and new aunt's taking of wafer and wine, I stood too, but as I edged to the aisle, my new aunt's father palmed my chest so hard that I fell back into the pew. He shook his finger in my face. "No Cath-o-lic."

Whereas Catholicism was another force that denied me, Buddhism fed me, quite literally. The monk, ông thầy, lifted the orange drape of his robe's sleeve so it would not dip into the aluminum trays of cá kho tộ, cơm, canh chua—all made vegetarian, in the way of Buddha. My mother and I sat under a tree and ate, the flavor deep and peppery in tofu's mimicry of flesh.

Those bites, under the monk's smiling nods, wove together all my cheesy t-shirts of wolves howling at the moon and bears pawing at honeycombs, the endangered animal fact cards I eagerly awaited in the mail, the hamster I smuggled on a plane. All of this coalesced into my decision to become a vegetarian.

With my dad's child support checks, I fed myself boxed mac and cheese, microwaveable bean and cheese burritos, and Teddy Grahams. At school, I hovered around the cheerleaders' lunchtime practice and entertained their body talk until they discarded half-eaten sandwiches, which kept me full until I went to work as a cashier at Target, adjacent to a Taco Bell, whose employees learned my orders of Mexican pizzas. "No meat," the drive thru speaker crackled back.

It took time to educate myself. I read pamphlets about the geopolitical and environmental impacts of the meat industry and found a deeper cause—political and spiritual—for going vegetarian. The foods I ate were a way to marry Buddhism and punk rock, to unify seemingly disparate parts of my life. Here was something that could be mine.

The shine was temporary. My mother was not proud as I thought she would be, since she'd introduced me to this way at the temple. "Why you so picky," she said. "You not gonna eat my food? It's vegetarian. Just pork floss. In Việt Nam, we eat what we have. Eat. Eat. Ugh. Fine, starve then." I didn't mention it to her again, just ate around the dried, shredded pork she sprinkled on top of my rice, forked to the side the chunks of chicken and, when she wasn't looking, slid them over to my brother and sister's plates. My mother had taught me not to waste. When my uncles teased me for eating only "rabbit food" that made me weirder and less a part of the family meals, I ate silently, accustomed to feeling that I deserved shame.

I began to obsess about what I ate. I was determined to whittle away at what my mother repeatedly bemoaned: I was so big that she gained half of her body weight while pregnant with me. This turned into counting calories, and I got down to 500 a day. While babysitting my toddler sister one day, I got up off the couch to chase her in her purple Teletubbies costume and immediately blacked out and knocked my head in a straight fall to the tile floor. When I came to, I saw her tiny face hovering over mine, her brow furrowed in worry underneath her purple felt hood. I would stay vegetarian for fifteen more years until I visited Việt Nam for the first time and did not want to refuse people who offered me meat, but I stopped denying myself calories that day. I didn't want to die in front of my sister.

I tried to eat myself back to life with equal obsessive fervor. On my mother's couch, I palmed handfuls of chips until I could shake into my mouth the crumbs at the bottom of the bag, and I gorged Tina's microwaveable burritos that were never heated all the way through. I only got up during

CHAPTER 12

MTV commercial breaks to pause the spin of VHS tapes that I methodically recorded on. Eating was future-focused, and if I was headed there, then I needed to save so that I wouldn't forget. During one binging-toward-future session, the TV was hijacked by breaking news of the shooting at Columbine High School. Pixelated footage of the teenaged shooters wearing black trench coats compelled my mother to pause her slipper shuffle from sweeping, dusting, and toddler-chasing. She stood at the back of the couch, directly behind me, where I could not see but only feel her presence. I chewed my chips more slowly, quietly, waiting. It felt as though my throat was beginning to close. "Wearing all black," she said suddenly. "Like you." A pause, and then, "You think this is cool?"

"No," I said. "This is terrible—" and I can't remember what else I said to reassure her enough to go back to her housework. In her absence, her words weighed heavy. I was wounded by the fact that—even though the vegetarianism, the punk, the black was all rooted in the spirituality that I learned from her—she could and would see the worst in me. My own mother knew I wouldn't eat a chicken but thought I was capable of murdering my classmates.

That's when I started picking apart the wholeness that the temple's fortune sticks had predicted. Vietnamese astrology treated you as a whole, destined, with predetermined dates of when and what was lucky. The numbers I shook out in prayer dictated everything I did, including the number of steps I counted until starting the number cycle again—a chant for the everyday. My mother had taught me to survive by fitting in, by keeping my hair straight and not too long not too short, by speaking without an accent, by smiling in pictures but not showing teeth. With one piece of my body at a time, I challenged her assimilation-to-survive aesthetic. I had been doing this all along anyway, trying to look more white, more brown, more this, less that. This was just a new iteration, a story untold—something to distract. I was extra.

Fishnets diamonded my legs under PE shorts; my sloppy needlework stitched band and animal rights patches onto my sweaters that covered my bulging chest and my arms, laced and dotted with self-inflicted cuts that tested my edges of pain, and then stirred my maternal will to survive by nursing my own wounds; six-dollar pots of Manic Panic dyed my hair alternating colors of the rainbow, which stained the yellow towels for which I had developed an intractable obsession. I ripped and resewed my mother's old maternity clothes into skirts, belts, and chokers. While I fixated on specific yet inane details remaining the same, my body was all pieces that I could change and reassemble.

I turned blades to my hair, shaving the back, sides, chopping the top to spike. But I could not shave my head as much as I wanted to in order to free myself from the incessant preoccupation with my hair. My mother was haunted by memories of her grandmother shaving her head in mourning of her husband's death, so choosing baldness was prohibited. "Like someone die. Such bad luck," my mother wailed in mourning of my hair, so I was alone with the cool breeze on my scalp.

As much as shaving my head was taboo, the women in my family were all about altering their hair—dyeing, highlighting, perming, and styling—and drawing in or tattooing eyebrows. Modeled after my mother's insecurity-rooted vanity, I lost track of time in front of the mirror. I dug out pores and flexed facial muscles to ward off sag, but mostly I went to great lengths to tape off and tweeze out my eyelashes, squinting through my breath's fog on the mirror to focus on the white root as it exited my skin. It looked like the reverse motion of the microscopic footage of a sperm burrowing into the membrane of the egg. Sometimes I plucked my lashes in patterns of patches and over-tweezed my eyebrows into pronounced arches. My eyebrows became so thin and sparse that their absence only further emphasized the bulging largeness of my face. "Trán dô."

I colored in the spaces where my lashes and brows were supposed to be with eyeliner even though they sweated off during PE or my slow, meandering—no, stalling—walks home after school. I purloined half-used eyeliner sticks that were discarded into my mother's hatboxes full of cosmetics that she hoarded by purchasing a lipstick expensive enough to earn the free gift bag of samples, only to return the original lipstick and keep the giveaways. During her regular surveillance sweeps of my room while I was at school, she stole them back from me. She hid the hatboxes. She had been stolen from enough. Now me. Until I could afford to buy my own eyeliner at the

CHAPTER 12

drugstore, I avoided sleeping because closing my eyes rubbed off the eyeliner that I had on. With what I had, I did my best to camouflage these rituals of pain into the jagged, colorful punk aesthetic. While other teenage girls were Nairing and waxing and shaving first-sex pussies, I was struggling to give shape to my self-inflicted blankness.

As much as my mother disapproved of my changing look, she once gifted me an expensive pair of Dr. Martens creepers, thick-soled and marbled blue. I loved her gesture so much, but I was so worried to scuff them or to be seen as a rich kid that I never wore them. My guilt grew.

•

My dad was at once the opposite and the twin of my mother. Whereas my mom's bedroom was all mirrors and photographs of herself, my dad shaved in the dark.

"Don't cut yourself," I called into the bathroom.

"Seeing myself in the mirror would hurt more," my dad called back, quick like truth.

I am my parents' only biological child together. I was the one child, the unique combination of their DNA—the living reminder—of how they both hated themselves. I oscillated between their styles of expressing it—magnification and darkness.

At my mom's house, I religiously watched *Entertainment Tonight*, *Access Hollywood*, and *Extra*, and all awards ceremonies in which I could obsess over every star, from Mary Hart's hair to the silhouette of the gown on whatever supermodel adorned DiCaprio's arm. When I could sneak past my mom's insomniac slipper-shufflings around the house, I turned on Conan O'Brien's midnight monologues and, on near mute, strained to hear every word of the celebrities' interviews.

On Dad weekends, I branched out from the mainstream. Our ritual began with a stop to Tower Records to rent movies, big and squeaky in their plastic VHS cases. I began to wander. I slipped on headphones at each listening station, flipped through all of the music magazines, and browsed the CDs of the canon—The Ramones, Subhumans, Crass, and the new release from Rancid. My dad was the one who introduced me to The Ramones' movie *Rock 'n' Roll High School* when I was just a kid admiring PJ Soles in her pigtailed fangirl glory. These were my primers for navigating Tower, and that space introduced me to a whole new language, one that would lead me to other, much smaller record shops like Bionic in Huntington Beach and Noise Noise Noise in Costa Mesa. Although I was usually the only girl in there pushing past dirty leather jackets and scuffed skateboards, the record shop was my classroom. I left each visit with stacks of zines in which I read about the bands that became my high school soundtrack—Naked Aggression, Defiance, Nausea. I bought t-shirts to match my fandom for these bands. Wearing their merch made it much easier to visibly identify with a community, a sense of belonging I craved but was constantly failing because of an unrecognizability so much vaster than myself.

Just as I had deconstructed and reassembled myself, I cut out pictures from zines to collage my walls from ceiling to floor. To fill the empty in-between spaces, I photocopied magazines at the library and taped the black and whites of music, art, and fashion—from Hedy Lamarr to Angelina Jolie, Gregory Peck to Heath Ledger, and The Ronettes to Korn. My mother snuck into my room while I was at school to rip down a poster of the latter who, she told me later, "look like rapers." As much as I tried to make those four walls my own, it still did not feel like home. And my mother warned me that home could be nowhere else. The outside world, she threatened from her own experience, was dangerous. While it was true that whenever I walked to my friends' houses, men catcalled me at every corner, and my newly bright hair made me a more visible target, my mom's reminders of these outside threats only served to make me more anxious than safe. On the back of the door, she did her own decorating: news stories about identity fraud with her note scrawled, "Don't let mail sit in box," kidnapping and rapes, lists of reasons people got parking tickets, and the verbal warning that needed no posting: "You friends not your family. No one love you like me."

We began to fight harder, throwing things at each other, yelling then silencing, and my mom wrote pages-long letters about how much I hurt her. "I love you because I have to. You're my daughter. But I don't like you."

That particular fight, and I can't even remember what it was about, sent me shuttling to people's couches—my dad's for a while, then my aunt

CHAPTER 12

and uncle's, and then my friend Carolina and her mom Bella welcomed me to stay in their home for the rest of the summer. Because kindness and generosity radiated from them naturally, I don't think they realized they were saving my life.

Bella fed me her delicious homecooked food, hugged me tight, told me I was smart, and showed me what love could feel like. Bella yelled at Carolina and her brothers, only for them to laugh, which made her laugh too. "Little shits," she called them while smiling. It was an intimacy, a safety, that I envied.

My dear friend Carolina—all light and laughter and love—had a brother named Rafa—all tattoos and smoking and angst, so exactly the kind of picture my mom would tear up—whom I started dating when I was fifteen. He didn't say much but was a vegetarian too. Our courtship was pretty much just him telling me he was proud of me for going meatless. And then we were together.

Rafa was the drummer in a neighborhood punk band called Solution for Ignorance—a name I always laughed at—and they practiced in his garage, which became a community space—the opposite of my mom's emotionally enforced barricades. In that garage, I shared a couch with white boys who called themselves Stinky Nuts the Pirate, Poop, and James whose ordinary name was counterbalanced by his realistic zombie FX makeup. They talked a lot about anarchy and made fun of me and Carolina for being the only ones of the group enrolled in high school. Once they saw me reading a book on the couch in the garage, and after all the heckling, I kept my books hidden away in a bag covered in sloppily sewn band patches. Punk culture was making me question and crave learning, and I never pointed out that Rafa and his friends' talk of anarchy was just another subscription to an ideology that kept them from thinking for themselves.

Everything was "fuck it." I hadn't lost my mother enough to say "fuck it all" with conviction. As much as I tried to distance myself from her and what she wanted for me, I always felt the responsibility of our history to try and unfuck things.

At first, because we were just kids transforming childhood spaces into our own, we befriended a rich girl who wore designer bondage pants and got her hair bleached and spiked at a salon. She had a Disneyland annual pass, so we licked the reentry stamp on her hand to transfer it to our own, before the Magic Kingdom began requiring tickets and reservations and retinal scans and a blood pact to reenter the park. Under the spinning rockets in Tomorrowland, we sipped peppermint Schnapps out of souvenir Mickey mugs, smoked glowing cherries of cigarette butts in the tree-covered recesses flanking Sleeping Beauty's castle, and shouted punk renditions of "It's a Small World."

Before the Disneyland Resort renovated all of surrounding Anaheim, Harbor Boulevard at Katella Avenue was rough. Once, my friends and I were supposed to meet up with a guy who could get us booze. We crossed Katella to a rundown seedy '60s motel, called the Sun or something else ironic, and as we knocked on the door of his room, a sex worker came out of the adjacent room and approached me. Her breath still warm and musky, she told me she liked girls too and asked if I wanted to be with her for an hour. With a discount. It wasn't that she was a sex worker or a woman, but something about the rush of her hustle—that she hadn't even closed the door on her john before marketing to me—that really eroded my Disney buzz.

Our booze hook-up finally opened the door and ushered us into the room. Inside, a guy was duct-taped to one of the flimsy motel chairs, gagged and struggling. As quickly as we were ushered in, we backed out. I'm pretty sure that's the last time we went to Disneyland together.

Instead, we became seatbeltless freeway flyers, packed into vans that our licensed friends borrowed from their suburban parents: Chain Reaction and The Doll Hut in Anaheim, The Glass House in Pomona, The Showcase Theatre in Corona, some random bar in La Habra, and Koo's Café in Santa Ana, where Rafa's band often played. One night at Koo's, a middle-aged man in a beret and cargo shorts approached to bum a cigarette from my friend Katie who had a gravitational pull on people. Not me.

Immediately, I judged him. I thought he was some creep with a young punk girl fetish to relive his '80s youth. But he talked to us in a very TV-dad way. "I come here to share a meal, a story, a laugh. It's important to be good to each other." Katie, much more open-hearted than me, nodded and

CHAPTER 12

chatted with him. Taught to always distrust strangers, I stood back, smoked. When we parted ways, he told us, "The *OC Weekly* interviewed me." My interest piqued by reading, I asked, "About what?"

"You gotta read to find out."

On my next visit to Tower Records with my dad, sure enough I saw Mark on the cover holding a cardboard sign that said, "Homeless in Orange County." He'd never mentioned that, but it all made sense—sharing a meal at Koo's, his clothes. In the article, he detailed how he'd become a person who was homeless. Decades later, his story is still imprinted on my memory.

He'd been a contractor—house, truck, business—and was living the typical suburban life that people think of when they hear Orange County. He and his wife had a son, but their marriage didn't work out, so they co-parented. When their son was three or four, his wife started dating again, and a long-term boyfriend moved into the house they once shared. A year or so into their cohabitation, his wife called him, hysterical. The house was on fire. It turned out that the boyfriend had been sexually abusing the son, and that day did so much damage to the boy's body, he panicked and lit the child on fire to cover the evidence. The flames could not be controlled. "I lost everything," he explained in the article.

That article would become one of the many reads that changed me. I had to check my judgments. Of others and myself. The thoughts that drove me to pull my hair were insignificant compared to the tragedies Mark suffered. In comparison, hairpulling was not a problem, just a thing I did, just a part of me and so maybe it was fine to keep plucking. I'd been raging at my mother for things that were big between us, but we were small in scope. We only used fire to cook and pray.

•

The first Asian American punk rocker I met called himself Troll. The summer I lived in Bella's home, my patient and devoted dad drove me and Rafa out to San Bernadino for a huge showcase revival, including T.S.O.L. and Vice Squad. My dad had introduced me to concerts—Little Richard, John Fogerty, Joan Jett, and countless others.

My dad's always on White People Time, so we got there super early and were left in the roiling heat before the venue opened its doors. Rafa knew everyone. In part because of his band's network, but he also just knew how to approach people with ease, as if they'd lived on the same street their whole lives and he was just bumming a cigarette like it was any other Tuesday. I admired his ability to be himself and connect. It always felt like I was a step behind his elbow, reticent because of the fears, doubts, and insecurities my mother had seeded in me. We were walking along the sidewalks of the surrounding neighborhood looking for shade when we approached a van with its sliding door open. I looked down and wanted to keep walking, but Rafa stepped up to the van and, in his way, lifted his chin and said, "Hey, man. Can I get one of those?"

"Yeah, man! Come on in. I'm Troll."

Troll was round, except for the foot-tall green and purple trihawk and the studs on his leather jacket. His girlfriend, a white girl, sat next to him, her bony knees pressed together, and a big pregnant belly bulged on her lap. She dragged a cigarette and stared out the greasy tinted windows. Rafa and Troll shot the shit while they smoked and sipped Coronas.

Rafa and I often fought, and our relationship showed me that I hurt people as much as they hurt me. But he also reminded me of my mother in the way that he always came to my defense, at least in front of other people. They were the only ones who could come down on me because, in their way, they loved me.

Rafa asked for a beer for me when Troll didn't even acknowledge me. When Rafa handed me the bottle, Troll said, "What's wrong with her?" Rafa redirected the conversation and, because Troll continued to ignore me, I pored over his face. He was dark-skinned with pockmarks and a wide, round nose. His potbelly and the way he pronounced "th" like "d" reminded me of my uncles. The more I found familiarity in him, the more I wanted him to recognize me. "So why 'Troll'?" I heard Rafa ask.

"Because I'm dat fuckin' ugly, man!" His girlfriend snorted.

Rafa turned to her. "When's the baby due?"

Troll interjected. "Any day now. Hope it's not ugly as me."

"It's half me too," she said.

CHAPTER 12

Rafa looked at me and then, "You know, you shouldn't be smoking. It's bad for the baby."

"Thanks, asshole. I stopped smoking crack. I'm not giving up cigarettes." Rafa looked to me again, and I started to feel nauseated.

"It's just really bad," he said.

"Don't fuckin' tell my girl what to do," Troll said.

I leaned out of the open door of the van and braced myself to throw up.

"She a poser or something?" Troll asked. His girlfriend snorted again, and I could hear the paper of her cigarette singe.

"Let's go." I felt Rafa's hand on my back, and we were out in the sun again.

I avoided Troll's trihawk bobbing in the pit and watched from the side of the stage as Rafa threw elbows through the crowd and lassoed his shirt above his head. I felt hot breath on the back of my neck and turned to see my people's high cheekbones and side leer staring back at me. I sidestepped away and saw that he was wearing a polo shirt and dark jeans, topped by a haircut about ten years out of style. How he'd come to a punk show full of leather and spikes and chains, I wasn't sure. Between him and Troll, I felt that worlds were blending and I wasn't sure how to navigate. I turned back to the stage where Beki Bondage was leaning into the pit of cycloning hormonal dudes. I had my own side leer going on and saw in my peripherals the Vietnamese guy approach me again. This time, he lifted my skirt and his fingertips brushed the crease between my butt cheek and upper thigh before I pushed his chest and sent him flying across the sweat-streaked, beer-puddled dance floor. He knocked into a trio of mohawked head-bobbers and they pushed him further into the crowd. Before he disappeared into the mob, I thought I saw his cheeks redden and, for a moment that I've experienced too many times—however fleeting and misplaced—*I* was the one who felt bad.

As Vice Squad's set ended, Rafa emerged from the pit shirtless and reeking of beer, his shoulders braced and the look in his eyes wild and ready. Part of my mother's survival tactics was still embedded in me because, to this day, I'll struggle and squirm and suffer before admitting that I need help or that I'm scared or in pain. But I craved more action than just staying there by the edge of the stage, so I appealed to Rafa. "Hey," I said, pulling him close so I could see the change in his eyes. "Some fucking asshole just grabbed my ass."

There's something about dudes that I've always so envied. In all the times that I've wanted to escape my body, I've often envisioned myself as a man. I fantasized that when I got mad, no one would tell me to calm down or be quiet. My mother couldn't remind me anymore, "Only if your husband let you." My body wouldn't have to cage that wild.

Head on swivel, Rafa was running into the crowd before I could even finish describing the guy who, I'd left out, was Vietnamese. Simply telling Rafa that I'd been violated made me feel safer, and his immediate leap to action made me feel his love for me and mine for him. Before T.S.O.L.'s set even began, Rafa was in front of me again, sweating and stinking. "The little Asian dude, right?" I nodded. He sucked his teeth. "That guy's a little pussy. He won't bother you again."

"What'd you do?" I asked, but Rafa was already preoccupied with the roadies setting up the stage. "Double bass drums, babe!"

"What did you do to him? Did you hit him?" I wasn't sure what answer would have made me feel better, but his response did not: "Nah, not worth it. He's just a little Asian dude."

I deflated twofold and watched as Rafa and all the other guys revolved around the pit, their voices heaving together as they sung along with the chorus, "I wanna fuck the dead!"

•

Back at school for my junior year, I could see the color lines shifting and thrumming. Now that I had been with Rafa for over six months—some kind of threshold of commitment in teenaged time—and I was fully versed in the language of punk music and fashion, I was corralled into the group that circled on the grass in front of the administration building as some kind of antiestablishment demonstration, though all it got us was detention and Saturday School slips for breaking the dress code. All these white kids weren't really protesting anything; they just wanted to be acknowledged

CHAPTER 12

for their anger and to stand out as different. There was a hepatitis scare at school because a student had contracted it while vacationing in Asia, so my infected-since-birth self shifted into lo pro mode and just tried to blend in with these clean, white kids only pretending to be dirty.

There was a subset of straight-edged boys who wore matching Dickies hooked to suspenders and fedoras. Their fashion, coupled with their commitment to a drug- and sex-free lifestyle, made them inconsequential to me. Except for one. In English class, I sat one seat behind him in an adjacent row—the perfect angle to catch the baldness of his eyelid. Mr. Sullivan's lectures on *A Tale of Two Cities* went underwater for me as I fixated on the changing topography of this boy's eyelid. As soon as a blond stub would grow in, he'd tilt his fedora down like Humphrey Bogart and tug it out, flicking it onto and then brushing it off of his French Revolution worksheet. Like in so many other instances, I admired this white boy's boldness of pulling in public and envied that no one commented on it. I was torturing myself by refraining from the ever-present urge to pluck over the course of the entire seven-hour school day, and still football players teased my lashlessness pronounced in microscope activities in biology. So fuck it. This boy's brazenness pushed me over that threshold. During a test, I left bubbles empty as I pulled at a thick stub whose root I could feel pulsing and wet under the skin. It didn't want to come out. I pressed my index finger and thumb harder and yanked the lash out. It was thick and coarse, and I felt the fleeting rush of excising this hair and leaving behind a hole in the skin of my eyelid, cold to the air and itchy from the break. That high, though, crashed when I saw the black smudges on my thumb and index finger. My pull had worn off the eyeliner that I used to fill in my blank eyelids to avoid stares and whispers. I did not have the eyeliner with me. I would have to go through the rest of the school day knowing that my bald eyelid was exposed, that my ruse would not convince anyone that it was an artistic makeup choice and not a cover-up of a deeper mental illness. That smudged eyeliner was one of many lessons about how I could never emulate white males whose privileges I envied and hated.

The most self-important of them all was a two-person branch of the punk crew that joined halfway through the school year. One was a six-foot-plus tall lanky guy who introduced himself as "Jason Rebel" as he tipped his cowboy hat and hooked his thumb on his Confederate flag belt buckle. He openly claimed "White Power" and spat chewing tobacco into a crinkled Coke can. His sidekick, or maybe his leader, was a silent mohawked yet beanied guy. He never looked me in the eye and once called Rafa a beaner, yet girls across social strata swooned for him, thinking his clenched jaw made him look sexy and strong. They found his silence intriguing. I just thought it was creepy. Years later, I found out that he murdered a cab driver. Hate crime.

The way that white supremacy amoebaed into punk at my school was how it was happening at shows, in other cities, throughout history. The racist entanglement and co-opting of a generative, equity-minded movement gave me more to fight for and helped me define survival in my own way.

One day, my mom picked me up from school. She'd gotten mad at me for taking too long to walk home. Rafa would meet me midway and we'd linger in the parks along my route to the house. She made me wait for her in front of the school, where everyone could see. As she pulled up, she yelled at me through the open passenger window and waved me to her in the way that Vietnamese moms do, as if they're shooing you away. I hurried to limit how many classmates witnessed this.

The next day at lunch, one of my classmates, a Puerto Rican guy who turned me on to the gem that is *The Golden Girls* ("Blanche is so funny, girl," he'd laugh and swat my arm as if we were watching it right then), said, "I saw your mom."

I deflected, "*Your* mom."

"For real," he said. "I'd never seen her before. When she picked you up yesterday she was all, 'Ching chong ching.'" He swatted my arm like we were talking about Sophia and Dorothy. "Such a gook!" The survival instinct that my "gook" mother had instilled in me surfaced and I stabbed my Bic ballpoint into his arm. A perfect blue hole. He yelled and I saw in his eyes that he wanted to tell someone. "Don't be a pussy," I said.

After school, my mom drove me and my siblings through the Taco Bell drive thru. "No beef," my mom yelled into the speaker.

I crunched layers of beans, cheese, and tomato in between crispy tortillas as I did my homework at the dining table instead of my room. In the

CHAPTER 12

evening, I sat next to my mom while she watched *Wheel of Fortune*. She overenunciated letters, "Mmmmm" and "Arrrrrrrr," then doubted herself, "Oh no! Wait, con ơi," she turned to me, "how you use 'F'?"

•

A few years later, I sat with my mom watching a short-lived *Fear Factor* knockoff, *Dog Eat Dog*. The blonde bombshell hostess introduced the contestants to increasingly humiliating challenges, from chugging bull balls to being Houdini-chained and dunked into a whale-sized tank of water or Kool-Aid or anything. We watched together while eating snacks, and I tried to sate my hairpulling urges by plucking grapes from their stems, though it was never the same if I wasn't inflicting pain on myself. As my mom click-shelled pistachios, the hourglass with red lips introduced Troll. I did not tell my mom that I had met him. "Ai-ya," my mother sighed with salty breath. "Hair," she said and shook her head. Troll's trihawk was still charged as high as it had been that day Rafa and I met him in the van. My dye had since grown out, so now I was back to my natural chestnut with only tips of faded purple and green. In that time, Rafa and I had inevitably broken up. He disappeared for a while and then returned as if nothing had happened. His head was shaved and he wore a clean white t-shirt and jeans when he drove me to Jack in the Box. He inhaled a Sourdough Jack and winced when I declined. "I got over that whole vegetarian thing," he said, dismissing what had brought us together. After that, he never knocked on my window late at night again. I heard later that he had a baby, a son.

So I had no one to share my awe of Troll's fifteen minutes of fame, some punk rocker on a mainstream stage. When the hostess asked him to introduce himself, he didn't mention anything about being a dad. Just whooped and yelled, "I'm crazy! Let's do this!"

Staring at the screen, my mother said, "Asian parents, we don't like this." She switched over to *Wheel of Fortune*. I lay my head on my mother's frail shoulder. As much as I'd resisted, she was with me all along. She clicked her tongue. "'Before and After,' oh trời!" She clasped her hands in prayer.

PHOTO ALBUM 2

Even when I was still a kid, I always welled up when I saw pictures of my younger self. I've embarrassed myself many times around a photo album. As others laugh and tell stories, I am silently holding back tears.

I've realized that I'm grieving all the things I could have been if not for fear or self-loathing or the voices of others that I've mistaken for myself. The photographs pull the sadness up and out of me because I am grieving who I could have been. I'm grieving, too, that I'm still just as sad as I remember being when the picture was taken, that it wasn't just temporary.

The seed of this mourning is the fear that my self has been irrevocably lost because no one, including myself, has been able to traverse the walls I've built to fully know or remember.

I'm always proven wrong. Recently, Bella messaged me a photograph taken by a mutual friend Carolina and I had in high school. She is now a lauded visual artist whose powerful work showcasing women's politicized bodies has been featured in magazines, galleries, and the streets of Los Angeles. Back when we were fifteen, she decided to see and photograph me. Somehow, that makes me sad too. The grief is also in the moments of finally getting what I wanted and needed. As I analyze the image of my teenaged self more closely, I grieve all the ways that my body lays bare my lifelong struggles.

      Brows as negative
    Space, tweezed chola-thin, empty
     Trán dô, no expressed

    Feeling. Wayward, lashless eyes
    Drawn in—a darkening slate.

Unhealed arm contorts
Into the flaking tree bark
Elbow thrusting at

The eye that sees you posing
From broken to ornament.

        Play music, be her—
      what I was Supposed to do.
       Twist away, wrist. Reach

      For the flame that hailed police,
      Worried light would become fire.

PHOTO ALBUM 2

Taffeta and lace
Float softly yet bind tightly
The body I bear

Usually sweatered, hiding
Scarred skin and shrinking from view.

River corpse–soft legs
Envy daughters' muscled calves
Practiced, free, strong.

On tree roots, they numb and lose
Balance—tilting to, away.

CHAPTER 13

SLEEPER

In Ross Gay's aptly named essay, "Fishing an Eyelash: Two or Three Cents on the Virtues of the Poetry Reading," he writes, "Books do not, mid-poem, reach the forefinger and thumb into one's mouth to gently fish out an eyelash. There are multiplicities within a human body reading poems that a poem on a page will never reproduce. In other words, books don't die. And preferring them to people won't prevent our doing so."

By my senior year of high school, I stopped going to punk shows and spent weekends reading the books that my dad bought for me. Many of them were comic book series like *The Sandman* and *Kabuki* and *Johnny the Homicidal Maniac* that I got on our summer trips to Comic-Con in the days before you had to wait in line for a week to get into Hall H. One Saturday night, I attempted to disrupt a regular bout of hairpulling insomnia by creasing the soft spine of the latest airport paperback bestseller, Lorenzo Carcaterra's *Sleepers*. I'd read in entertainment magazines that Brad Renfro—another iconic good-bad boy, rest in peace—had been cast in the film adaptation, so I needed to read the book to learn all I could about his character and, in that lonely part of my mind, get closer to him.

The novel surprised me with how engrossing it was, and the page-turning plotline was more satisfying than any dissociative tunnel I'd Aliced into. I

CHAPTER 13

kept reading until dawn broke and, most satisfying of all, relished in more than a few hours of not pulling my hair. A book had given my body a break from my mind. I felt accomplished. I felt healing.

I heard my mother's slippers shuffle to my door. Her tongue clicked and she muttered, "Doesn't turn off the lights. Wasting money." She threw open the door, and when she saw that I was not only awake but reading, her rage boiled over and she shuffled right back out of the door, which she slammed behind her.

I stayed in bed to avoid the tension but also to keep reading *Sleepers*, which I finished by squinting through my fingers that my mother sent back to tugging eyelashes. Because I read the rest of the book while plucking, I couldn't remember the ending. Every pluck wore away at my remembering.

> *"She disliked anything that reminded her that she had been seen sitting thinking" (Woolf 68).*

Though my non-hairpulling streak did not last long, that unintentionally punny sleepless night of reading *Sleepers* cemented that books were my escape. Even though no one had talked to me about continuing my education after high school, I got into college on a fluke, one that actually ran quite contrary to the tenets of academia. Despite having pulled my C average up to straight A's starting in the latter half of my junior year, I still in no way compared to the other students (the majority of whom were Asian *or* white) in my AP classes who had four-plus years of immaculate transcripts and a long list of student club leadership and community service. It was the mandatory Practice SATs that saved me.

On the front of the score sheet where you had to tediously bubble in your name, you also had to select specific colleges to which you wanted your scores sent. Peering over my friend's shoulder, I saw that he had filled in Cal State Long Beach. Though I'd never heard of the school, or any school for that matter (save for the Harvards and Yales and other such fictional universities in '80s comedies), I recognized the city name because it was just across the bridge from San Pedro, and I had spent a summer living there with one of my uncles when my mom told me, "I love you, but I don't like you," and then, in cliché break-up fashion, "I think we're better off apart."

I filled in that bubble just so that my sheet would not be blank and I wouldn't give away my listless lack of foresight and ambition to the majority of my classmates whose parents had helped them map out options in higher education. Based on my scores, CSULB sent me a letter encouraging me to apply, which I did. After all, the cashier job I had at Target was not working out well. One of the managers had told me I had a serious medical condition called No Personality-itis, and a customer carrying a toddler became so angry when I told her she had to take returns to the Guest Services desk that she yelled at me and called me a "stupid fucking retard" right in front of her baby.

Surprised, confused, and a little scared, I took my CSULB acceptance letter to show my mother, whom I bumped into in the hallway as she was on her way out. "I got into college, Mom," I said and handed her the letter. She glanced at it briefly. "Okay," she said in a downward slope as if the word had a dấu huyền. "Good, so what you want me to say?" She didn't wait for an answer, of which I had none, and shuffled past me toward her errands in Little Saigon.

It wasn't until later, after the sting of rejection had worn off, that I remember I *had* heard of CSU Long Beach. It was the college my mother had wanted to go to for nursing but was not able to afford. Because she was raising me. Instead she had cobbled together enough credits at various community colleges to earn a nursing license, sometimes having to bring me to class with her. I had wounded her with my acceptance letter.

By the time I figured out how to get to freshman orientation, all of the English classes were full, so the counselor, taking each of us in the long line by number rather than name, enrolled me in Black Studies 100. "It'll be the same," he lied.

If my mother had asked about school, I wouldn't have told her. "Stay away," she always told me about Black people, whom she'd often described, with a grimace, as "đen thui." Anti-blackness polluted all my cultures. When my dad asked, "What's Black Studies?" I didn't know how to answer.

CHAPTER 13

Of many confessions, one is that I didn't want me to take Black Studies either. Because I had not yet learned how inextricably tied our histories were. I had yet to see myself as subject *and* object.

At the college bookstore, I found the assigned textbook: Zora Neale Hurston's *Their Eyes Were Watching God*. My dad waited in line with me and paid for all of my books, and all of the ones that would be assigned in my following semesters of what became a string of three degrees. It was just as he'd done with all my childhood books, series after series of chapter books that kept me out of trouble, as well as *Sleepers*. His twelve dollars gifted me a paradigm-shifter, one of my most worn spines. Yet, the markings in it are only from that first semester of college—light, timid pencil underlines of Hurston's words that reverberate to my core still today. I'd worried that the consistency attested to lack of growth, of learning, but I learned in the Black Lives Matter protests in the years thereafter that it was truth.

> *"Janie full of that oldest human longing*
> *—self-revelation" (Hurston 7).*

I've held on to all the papers from that Black Studies course, keeping the trail that singed and curled away from the burning fingertips of those who came before us.

The first day of class was my eighteenth birthday. Because I was the annoying paradox of yearning but refusing to be seen, I did not release this information from my tightening throat during the icebreaker roll call. I offered something unmemorable and Professor Fuller, all grace and ease at the podium, moved on to the next name. I was relieved when another Asian student named Kevin introduced himself by saying that he signed up for the class because he thought Black people were funny. Professor Fuller's body stiffened. "Funny, huh?" And she unleashed. "Because we're easier to tame if we're 'jus' tellin' jokes to dah massa'?" She pointed to all the Black men at their desks, "Are you funny? Do you want to get up and do a song and dance to make Kevin laugh?" In the first fifteen minutes, she had drawn us all together in spotlighting racism. She was not afraid to call it out. Her throat was open, her voice truthful. I covered my smile.

Then, Professor Fuller lined us up. Chalk dusted the back of my sweater as I tried to lean out of everyone's view. Depending on our answers to her questions, we would take a step forward or stay in place.

"Did you grow up in a house?"

"With two parents?"

"Does your mother have a college degree?"

"Take a step for every generation you can trace back on your family tree."

"Does anyone in your family have a criminal record?"

Questions later, I remained with my fingertips on the chalk shelf, Chantal next to me but looking straight ahead at our classmates standing in a bar graph of privilege.

> *"'us colored folks is branches without roots and that makes things come round in* queer ways'" *(Hurston 16).*

My throat constricted until it was hard to swallow. I wanted to drop the class after that exercise. But I didn't know you could do that. And then the professor kept me by writing to me.

On an in-class writing titled "The Gap Exercise," my eighteen-year-old self wrote:

> I think the purpose is to show the privileges people receive based on who they appear to be, and even though I'm proud of my family and my combined cultures that have created a unique upbringing for me, my first impression of "stepping back" was to be embarrassed or ashamed that my parents aren't together or they dropped out of school or don't speak the best English. I think that physically being "behind" others and "stepping back" has a psychological and esteem effect, like even though we're all people in the same place & world, sometimes it feels like we're not all running fairly in the same race, it's just harder for a lot of people for a lot of the wrong reasons.

CHAPTER 13

Professor Fuller responded:

Your flow is engaging, illustrating great potential for focused intellectual thought! Keep it up!

Here was a response to my ideas, my self. Professor Fuller, in just two exclamation points, made me feel seen in ways I didn't realize I'd been craving for all the years I'd only been written to in chastising letters from my mother.

I stayed in Black Studies 100. On the second day of class, we took, and failed, a diagnostic exam. "Like the slaves," Professor Fuller told us, "you will be brothers and sisters bound by sweat and blood. You will be responsible for each other's failures and be punished together." She put us "on the line" to show the devastation and power of how all those inequities we had confronted in the gap exercise can be, and was, all taken away. That day, in our new family, we wrote in repetition our own punishment:

Based on the test results, it is obvious that we are not taking this class seriously. Furthermore, the results illustrate that we have a lack of respect for the written word and our instructor. Accordingly, we are now officially on the line.

Based on the test results, it is obvious that we are not taking this class seriously. Furthermore, the results illustrate that we have a lack of respect for the written word and our instructor. Accordingly, we are now officially on line.

Chantal wrote the first email I ever received, which sounds like history now. She scheduled study sessions: "I'm not gonna let you drag me down," she wrote to all of us. Equally selfish and hopeful, I felt as if she were writing only to me. Bound by words, we huddled in the must of books trying to do different. Inevitably, Kevin failed a reading quiz, and we were all punished. Chantal complained. And we were all punished. I—we—had to write ad nauseum:

There are no weak links in the line. You are all chained together; if one falls, everyone falls.

It was the third week of the semester that 9/11 happened to us all. I was not in Professor Fuller's class, but another Gen Ed requirement theatre class (that I would fail, probably due to puppet trauma) when the news broke. The class and then the campus were evacuated by teams of police on foot, bikes, motorcycles, cars, helicopters, the whole cavalcade. News and military choppers hovered over our campus, with reports speculating that largely populated areas, especially college campuses, might be the next targets. Not yet having a cell phone and my own car, I waited on a concrete bench for my stepdad, who had been a boat person, to pick me up. We did not talk on the ride because we never spoke, but this day with good reason to only listen to the news on the radio.

Back at the house with my mother and young siblings, I watched the looped footage with one eye, while I watched my mother with the other. Frenetic, she busied herself in the kitchen, with the babies, with the broom. She kept moving. I could only imagine then, before I had learned enough, how it must have felt for her to feel that it was happening again. The explosions. The bodies. The uncertainty.

As the not-so-past had taught her, my mother had already stockpiled supplies for events like this. But we would need more, the news anchors warned us. Watching my girl-mother dart around just to keep moving, I tried to be helpful. I called my dad, who always had canned food in his truck in case of emergency. "Hi, Dad," I said, without mentioning the planes or the burning bodies or my school's evacuation. "What's the best kind of canned chili?" And then I went to buy Dennison's for my mother's shelves.

A week and a half later, the military industrial complex and capitalism (and 89-cents-a-gallon gas) urged us to return to our normal routines. Back on campus, I returned to classes without eyelashes, plucked to the corners where it was all dry pinch—all desert, no jungle. As was regular with a

CHAPTER 13

full-eye pluck, shame spirals numbed me into an emotional hangover. So I tuned out the Islamophobic buzzing about Pearl Harbor echoes and the word "evil" and Al-Qaeda.

For weeks, Professor helped us survive the line during new wartime with a series of recitations that began "Just for today":

Nov. 5th, 2001

Just for today, I will try to live through this day only and not tackle my whole life problem at once. I can do some things for 12 hours that would appall me if I felt I had to keep them up for a lifetime.

Nov. 7th, 2001

Just for today, I will be happy. This assumes that what Abraham Lincoln said is true that "Most people are about as happy as they make their minds up to be." Happiness is from within and not a matter of externals.

Nov. 12th, 2001

Just for today, I will take care of my body. I will exercise it, care for it, and nourish it along lines best known to modern science for keeping it healthy so that it will be the perfect machine for my will.

Nov. 14th, 2001

Just for today, I will strengthen my mind. I will learn something useful and will study something that challenges my mental ability. I will not be a mental loafer all day. I will read something that requires thought and concentration.

Nov. 19th, 2001

Just for today, I will be agreeable. I will look as well as I can, dress as becomingly as possible, talk low, act courteously, not withholding a word of praise, will not criticize one bit, not find fault with anything, and try not to regulate or improve anyone.

This was new. And not just for me.

Newspapers came. Journalists scribbled on notepads, which feels like history now, and camera apertures zoomed and clicked her at that chalkboard that had dusted my hands, recorded the rhythm of her words that went around and straight through me. They interviewed Chantal, our leader, and she cried. And I was envious.

> "'Us colored folks is too envious of one 'nother. Dat's how come us don't git no further than us do. [...] Us keeps our own selves down.'" (Hurston 39)

Chantal never returned my gaze. I began to worry that she thought I was studying her, fetishizing her. Maybe it was one of the many things I didn't know I could do. She befriended a bubbly white girl who asked her pointed questions about what it was like to be Black, and the other Asian girl in class who wore tank tops and glittery eyeshadow. I didn't know anything about them, but I was jealous that Chantal had let them into her circle and not me. All I had was a right eyelid that was beginning to hang out of symmetry with the left because I was reaching nearly a decade of dominant right-hand hairpulling.

The closest I got to Chantal was when I began dating one of our classmates, an Afro-Latino who everyone liked and whose virginity I was afraid to take. I didn't break up with him because I didn't know I could do that. I watched as she cornrowed and beaded his hair that clicked when, after Professor asked "Are y'all together?" he responded, "Like peas and carrots." Chantal laughed, and Professor Fuller smiled over her shoulder. Even witnessing proximity to their simultaneous reaction to my boyfriend's charm, I felt the dopamine surge of maternal approval. Longing, I watched our professor walk from class, her wet curls swinging and swishing over "That

CHAPTER 13

Booty" the other boys in class bumped fists over.

Knee to knee in Professor Fuller's closet-sized office I forced my throat open to tell her that she—the most educated person I'd then ever spoken to—made me want to be a writer, made me remember the journals packed away where my mother wouldn't find them. "Maybe," she said, "it's the Native American in me. Or maybe it's my roots to Africa." Her wrists curtained her hair behind her shoulders, and the light shone on her freckled nose. "But I think it's important to go back to what makes us." And, up until she said those words to me, I didn't know you could do that either.

It makes a kind of sense that my first full essay for Professor Fuller's class was a story about running: a mother and daughter bound by pain and survival, a father and daughter trying to fall in step, a history interrupted—the inertia of restless legs pounding the earth. The beginning of that story read:

> I was getting excited dressing Lizzie for school that day. I tried to forget about the girl who had been beaten in front of the market just last week. A prayer had been stitched into every inch of the fabric that I had taken from the big house where I cleaned. The fabric of the dress was a soft yellow to bring out the glow in my baby's eyes.

Among her piles of plastic bags of prescription bottles and perfume and nail polish, my bà ngoại would lay on our couch, just visiting, like she was always temporary, an arm draped across her forehead, her dagger-toenailed feet planted flat, knees swaying back and forth to the rhythm of hummed prayer, moving, moving all through the night, her body still on Việt Nam time.

They say that I sleep like her. Ready to run.

My story continued:

> Lizzie was being followed by a blur of angry white faces and a

barrage of broken glass. When I threw the door open I could hear Lizzie's panting and see the glisten of her tears. The mob of teenage boys chasing her was ranting something about her walking on the wrong side of the street. Each time Lizzie's worn shoes pounded the dirt, I wished for her to be in a better place. Suddenly, one of the boys clipped the side of Lizzie's head with an empty bottle. It seemed as though Lizzie fell in slow motion. My legs had never felt so heavy as they did when I ran to her that morning. My head was rushing with so many thoughts that the shouts of "whore mama" from the boys were muffled. I realized that I had not finished buttoning my uniform when I came out of the house. The boys seemed satisfied and laughed as they walked away triumphantly.

My kindergarten teacher had mocked my running around the sock ball diamond.

Squinting into the sun, I ran over classmates' shadows shivering with laughter. I imagined running wild and free like freckled Laura in *Little House on the Prairie,* to and away. My dad ran actual marathons—multiple—and his disappointment over the absence of my medals' ting bellowed in my ears. The running I did was inside: no numbers, no awards. The only time she saw it, my mom told me, only once, "You my wild horse. Always running."

. . . memories of the baby that had been ripped from me flashed through my mind. I had vowed to myself that I would never let a white man take one of my babies again. Watching Lizzie crying and bleeding, I felt as if they already had. I was overwhelmed with the thought that nothing would ever change.

> "She had an inside and an outside
> now and suddenly she knew
> how not
> to mix them" (Hurston 72).

CHAPTER 13

For our final exam, we shared a meal. I learned that mac and cheese didn't come from a box. I listened to the girls in the class cry for their brothers in gangs. Everyone but me shared about our grandmothers who passed down food and story. Chantal never looked at me, and I've since regretted taking it personally, of letting it be my swelling silence.

> *"The Stillness was the sleep of swords"* (Hurston 81).

Chantal hugged and cried into the hair of our professor. As I witnessed their moment of closeness, I filled with the knowledge that I had learned more than I could show, that I couldn't. But I'd also erred in waiting for belonging to come to me, in longing for something that wasn't mine because I was just beginning to learn how to see myself.

From my class notes:

Zora – Harlem Renaissance, criticized black female author.

Janie strong, gets to her roots "further into blackness." Everglades.

Falls in love.

Poetic, articulate.

Below, upside down:

Jade keeps safe & warm – believed to be in Asian cultures. It's always developing – strength & beauty.

People – human contact

Professor Fuller taught me how to look for our histories that had been differently colored but were inextricably braided—the knots, the clicks, the strengthening of adding another strand of story. And to recognize all the unseeable things I could never know that kept me staring at Chantal and kept her from looking back at me.

I failed all of my other classes that semester. But never did again, trying to make up for the things that weren't and invested everything into the book learning—the only part of my life—that was not fishing for eyelashes.

> *"She had found a jewel down inside*
> *herself and she had wanted to walk where people*
> *could see her*
> *and gleam it around" (Hurston 90).*

CHAPTER 14

THE CHRISTIAN AND THE QUAIL

During my second semester of college, my great-aunt Adell was hospitalized with leukemia. She asked me to cut her hair. Like my paternal grandmother, her sister, who had died from cancer more than a decade before, Adell's hair was Irish red and carefully curled into bouncy ringlets. They were reverberations of the Shirley Temple style she had grown up with. Like some kind of Asian pride protest, my hair vehemently rejected curlers and immediately dropped flat. Aside from my punk era dyeing, shaving, and spiking, I didn't have experience with styling hair, especially not in perfect ringlets. I was afraid to mess up the hairstyle that she'd had for nearly seventy years, since she was a teenager scrapbooking all the headlines of war that interned her Japanese American best friend to whom she wrote letters in tight curled script, to all the years she had been a loving mother figure to my dad and a grandmother to me. "No," I refused. "I can't."

She was disappointed. All I did with her hair was hold it back as she vomited from the chemotherapy.

CHAPTER 14

A few days later, my dad called to tell me her body was already hard.

"You look lonely," a voice above me said, "like you could use a friend." My butt was numb from the cold concrete bench on campus. The college girl was Asian too, but Korean. But smiling. "Yes," I surprised myself, "someone I love just died."

"I'm so sorry for your loss," she said. "Would you like to get some coffee?" I agreed because that's what I saw white college kids on TV doing. Could it be this easy to make new friends?

Over her coffee and my hot chocolate (because I'm a fucking kid), I accepted the paperback New Testament from my new Korean friend. My mother's warnings echoed, but Adell had been friends with those who were different from her—internment camp survivor Josephine, her husband's ex-wife, and just about everyone she met. Every Christmas she sent cards to all of these people. Her cards were homemade typewritten stories about her cats, my dad, and me with pictures of us, but mostly cats. She was a writer whose words kept people close. She taught me to like stories. I used one of the bookmarks she'd given me—a bunny whose ears flopped over the pages—in my new New Testament.

Despite my crippling dread of driving new places because of my anxiety of other drivers getting mad at me and the fear of giving into suicidal thoughts that would be easier to manifest behind the wheel, I drove into the armpit of LA for Bible study at the Korean girl's apartment where I forced myself to hold hands with her roommates in prayer. They talked about Jesus and saving, and I held my questions to myself. Then, other girls knocked, entered, and joined hands too. I was not the only one. The girl had corralled a whole group of sad-eyed benchsitters. I had not been chosen as a friend or anyone special. I felt that, like in the Bible, we were names on names on names.

Great-Aunt Adell was not religious, but she taught me saving of a different kind. One of her houses in Sedona, Arizona, was a museum to her travels across the world. Troll statues from Norway, tribal masks from Africa, trinkets from Japan and Oceania. A hallway bookcase housed volumes of her meticulously curated scrapbooks detailing every major event from the '30s through the '60s, and photo albums collected black-and-white pictures of her and our Irish ancestors, children's limbs blurring in impatience with cameras that required a hold and wait. Every wall was covered in pictures from all parts of her life.

During one springtime visit to this house, I heard Adell yodel from the bedroom, "My word!" I ran to her, worried her metal knees from a teenage car accident had buckled in that house on a hill of red rock. She was huffing and screeching at one of her cats whose tail peeked from under the bed. She couldn't bend down to see. I crouched and crawled to pull the cat out. A quail's plume poked out between its paws. I wrenched the cat's predator bones apart and cupped in the cage of my hands a warm, soft-downed baby quail.

My great-aunt waddled to the back door as quickly as she could, an "oh oh" with every step. The screen opened to a sharp vista—manzanita, prickly pear, banana yucca. Adell cooed and yodeled as if to her cats, the children she never had.

Red dirt powdering my toes, I squinted through sunlight. I heard the rustle before I saw the mother's plume and waddle, a covey of chicks shuffling puffs of red desert dirt behind her.

I flattened my knuckles, fingernails, to the ground, and the baby's feet tapped relief across my palm lines. Reunited, they flushed.

I smiled at my great-aunt. "We saved them."

"My word," she said again, and smiled back.

On the other branches of my family tree, my married-in aunt introduced me to her friend who had recently survived a surgery to excise a brain tumor. "She can hear the voices of the dead now," my aunt whispered. She introduced me to this new medium, a tall and exaggerated beauty, like something rendered from Tim Burton's imagination. Her heavy brow arched and lip curled back to ask, "Do you want to know?"

As we sat knee-to-knee, she channeled my great-aunt. I could picture Adell's curls shaking when the medium transmitted her message: "Don't even think about getting that tattoo across your stomach." The medium mimicked smoothing batter with a baking spatula, "You need to focus on filling the hole in your heart." She followed with how I would find someone to help fill that hole, and that when I marry I should wear a flower in my hair

CHAPTER 14

the way she saw when she travelled to Hawai'i. The medium closed with Adell telling her heaven isn't real, at least the way it's storied by Christians, but that she was safe and happy with her cats.

And then, her puzzle: Amid turquoise, coral, and malachite, you'll find yourself, hanging, protected in gold. The medium and I shrugged at each other.

I felt burned by the Korean Christian, and "Will you cut my hair?" was hounding my memory. I regretted not stepping up to trim Adell's curls and punished myself by removing all of my eyelashes. The thumb and index finger of my right hand were becoming calloused from my punishing pick and pull.

Though I was still silent in my college classes, my irritability (resistance) was frothing behind my lips. In one course, we read *The Tao of Pooh*. (You motherfuckers can only "mmmm" and nod at centuries of Asian philosophy when it's channeled through an English bear? A mid cartoon? Everyone knows Eeyore is the only good character in that shit.) For my local geography project in another class, I reported on the Vietnamese mythology murals in the parking lot of the Á Đông Supermarket off of Bolsa in Little Saigon. "Can you hold up that flag again?" my professor asked at the end of my presentation. "Notice how she didn't use the official flag of Vietnam," he said to the class as my arms were raised, "but the former South Vietnamese flag?" (You—Fu—Grrr—You better give me an "A" for this. But not because I'm *that* kind of Vietnamese. Just—Fuck! I mean, borders are constructions, so Geography? A requirement?) Aside from retaking a math class that shall not be named, a Counseling course rounded out my schedule. In one session, we took the Myers-Briggs Type Indicator test. This actually appealed to me. Maybe I could figure myself out. Introverted, Intuitive, Feeling, Judging (INFJ). The professor asked us to reveal our types by show of hand, and I was the only one. At her instruction, I read aloud that INFJs comprise about one percent of the population. The boys sitting around me snickered. (Fuck. Off.) The Extroverted, Sensing, Feeling, and Judging (ESFJ) attention-seekers thankfully pulled the spotlight off of me, and I slouched back into my desk to read more about my supposed "type." Among the suggested career paths was poet. (Ugh, rude.) Teacher. (And do this? Pass.) Priest/Nun. (Catholic bias much?) But something hit.

Seeking, I attended a class at a Buddhist temple not far from the house where we'd met for Sons of Norway. The class was intended for those interested in devoting their lives to becoming monks. The loneliness compounded by this new concentric grief made me believe that a monastic life was possible, if not destined for someone as incompatible with life as I felt. Maybe being sequestered in a temple with a shaved head would grant me some peace.

Two class sessions in, the question-and-answer portion of the class started grating on my nerves because, like in my university courses, the other students had clearly not done the reading and could not answer the teacher's questions. Even monks-in-training could be dumbasses. "Water!" I wanted to yell. "The answer is to be like motherfucking water!"

Though it wasn't the answer I hoped for, I knew that I was not fit for monkhood. I mean, I spent weeknights with my mother watching (with a disturbing level of self-hating investment) the early wave of makeover reality shows: *Are You Hot?* featuring Lorenzo Lamas's infamous laser pointing of thigh gaps and *Extreme Makeover*, which made Mẹ "ooh" and "aah" and sometimes laugh at the head-to-toe plastic surgery. Not so much inner peace.

During Adell's scheduled cremation, my dad and I were preparing for our trip to Sedona to inventory the items for her estate. On the table next to me, a lamp turned on and flashed long enough for me to choke down my silence and yell, "Dad! Dad! She's here!"

In Arizona, I struggled with how to estimate the value of Norse troll dolls that had real human hair, or to quantify the value of her scrapbooks' thick pages wrinkled by rubber cement—these books that taught me to save pictures, stubs, dried petals, fingernail crescents of red dirt to combat the loss (the burn of paper) on that other side of the family tree.

In her bedroom, her jewelry case shone with the veined colors of the earth. Among the gilded armbands and heavy Navajo rings, a thin chain hung a locket of me as an infant, protected in gold. I was just as Adell had told the medium where I would be.

Outside, I dusted off my knees and lifted my arms up to the desert wind that blew sand into my lashless eyes. During an earlier road trip to visit

CHAPTER 14

Adell while she was alive, my dad and I pulled over to a chain of roadside stands where clouds of powdered sugar blanketed fry bread and silver glinted around veined turquoise and coral bright and round as wet lychees. Feathers hung, swayed, in the wind. The jewelry artist sold me—had to sell me—a spiral that tailed into a droplet of turquoise. As we exchanged, the wind picked up, and she gave me—but didn't have to give me—this: "My grandmother used to say that when the wind blows, that's your ancestors all around you. And," she laughed, "pushing you around, too. So, when the wind blows, you're not alone." All this time, I'd been wary of bad winds that my mom spoon-scratched out of my back.

Then, a quail skittered from behind the house and paused, its plume weathervaning in the gust. The college girl's book never told this story, the way the quail peered at only me. "Hi," I said, and we saved and saved and saved.

CHAPTER 15

DEAR ANGELINA JOLIE

Dear Angelina,

    I think you'd like it if I got right to it. In a late '90s issue of *Rolling Stone*, a post–*Girl Interrupted* and pre–Billy Bob you posed in a white tank top thin enough to show the plum areolas circling your erect nipples. With one arm, you lifted the hem of your shirt to reveal the tattoos across your lower abdomen—one of which was a crudely inked black cross that, in the accompanying interview, you admitted was a cover-up for a former suggestively positioned long and active tongue. Your other arm was extended and on your inner forearm I read, "A prayer for the wild at heart kept in cages." Tennessee Williams, you told the journalist. And I told the librarian.

    I was eager to start Williams' collected works. The only other play I'd read was the ninth-grade mandatory slog that was *Romeo and Juliet*. In another high school English class, my teacher had assigned each of us the work of a poet whom she had selected based on our interests and personalities. She had paired me with Allen Ginsberg. I wasn't sure what to make

CHAPTER 15

of this pairing. I reread the poems describing oral sex with young men and trying to find in blowjobs my teacher's message about myself. Williams' caged wild hearts in *Stairs to the Roof*, however, would surely have answers. Your tattooed quote was promise enough. Act 1, Scene 1: "There is a glassy brilliance to the atmosphere: one feels that it must contain a highly selected death ray that penetrates living tissue straight to the heart and bestows a withering kiss on whatever diverges from an accepted pattern." Yes, you understood me.

When I was able to pull my eyes away from your nipples, I reread the portion of your interview in which you expressed your love for your ex-girlfriend Jenny Shimizu. The fact that she was Asian American made this fantasy feel all the more possible. But it was the part of the interview in which you confessed your history with self-harm, mostly cutting, that I memorized. You accepted it and had come out on the other side. From the red carpet, you didn't realize that you were helping me through it.

At nineteen, I had worked enough overtime in retail to save money to buy an airplane ticket to visit Jennifer who had moved back to Oklahoma during our freshman year of high school. My mom did not approve of the trip. She still hated Jennifer, whose mom had called the police to our house after overhearing that I wanted to kill myself. I was twelve. In the front yard, I assured the officer that everything was fine, but I could feel my mother glaring at me through the screen door, searing holes into the back of my head. "I'm fine," I said too many times.

I couldn't win, so I went to visit Jennifer anyway. I packed a bag of all-black clothes modeled after your style, not realizing how out of place I would look among Oklahoman girls' Daisy Dukes and farmer flannels tied into midriffs. Jennifer picked me up from the Will Rogers Airport in Oklahoma City. "Ugh, rush hour traffic," she said, steering with her knees as one hand flicked a cigarette and the other held a Diet Coke. I looked out the window and counted seven cars on the highway. Streets were not this empty, not even in the middle of the night, in LA. "That's why I can't live in the big city," she said. She sucked the cigarette with what the boys at school had called "DSLs," and I felt an involuntary twinge of jealousy because the fullness of her lips was closer to your own than mine.

We arrived in Altus, bordering Texas, where Jennifer's dad was an engineer at the Air Force base. The military base, it turned out, was the only thing that brought people to the town. One stoplight swung in a manure-scented wind. One of Jennifer's friends asked us if we wanted to go cow-tipping. "He'll have sex with you too," Jennifer whispered to me. "A California girl would be a big get for him." I played pool for the first time. I also went to a twenty-four-hour Walmart and was floored by how bustling it was at 2 a.m. and that we could buy guns and live goldfish and cookies and lotion all in one place.

The lotion we needed because of the other difference that sent me into Oklahoman cultural shock. While piercing was popular with every teenager clicking barbells against their teeth and every femme girl baring a dangling charm from her belly button, tattoo parlors were illegal. "The Church is real big out here," Jennifer explained as I unpacked in her studio apartment. "Real big." I began to feel self-conscious about all the black clothes you'd inspired me to buy. The God-fearing girls I'd seen in town wore a lot of pastel plaids and white denim. "I should probably add some color to my wardrobe," I said, always preemptively self-criticizing.

"Nah, it's cool. Black is classic. Big city. Badass," Jennifer assured me, as she always did since we met in sixth grade because I was always doubting myself and she, in all her generosity, was always loving me.

She gave me courage. "Well, my mom says black is my lucky color according to the year and date and time I was born," I said, always seeking validation from my culture. She nodded and squinted through a plume of her exhaled smoke. "And I've been reading a lot about Angelina Jolie and she—"

"Oh, I love her. So sexy. I wanna be sexy like her. You know, Brian told me my lips are like hers." She puckered and pouted.

"Yeah," I said. "She wears black and has all these tattoos. There's one from this book."

"We should get tattoos together!" Jennifer's excitement was infectious. My heart surged with the possibility of getting the very same Tennessee Williams quote that you had on your own body. "—like a matching Chinese symbol or something. Maybe 'sisters'? Or maybe—"

I loved Jennifer. In fact, I admired how brave she was, even though it meant that sometimes she cut me off with her readiness to act. Not being

CHAPTER 15

fully heard was familiar to me, and I excused it more with her because I wanted to be like her, to be able to meet new people and dive into new experiences. And just to feel enthusiastic. About anything. But I couldn't. I was fixated. I had to follow the line to its end.

Because tattoo parlors were outlawed, we ended up at the apartment of a friend of her boyfriend. He was learning to use a tattoo gun at home and was offering to practice on us for free. The last word was all we heard.

On a faded couch in a guy's apartment, I watched Jennifer's boyfriend get some pseudo-tribal spiral, placid-faced while small talking with the self-taught tattooist. Watching him so calm about getting something so meaningless to him got my nervous system pinballing.

Outside on the balcony, I paced what three to four steps I could while I sliced down every reassurance Jennifer offered me. "Prayer," I insisted, "sounds so Christian. I don't know anything about that. And 'wild'? Am I really wild? I haven't done half the things you've done. And should there be a comma between 'heart' and 'kept'? Does the pause sound more yearning? Or is it too long of a pause?"

All of my obsessive doubt and negativity did not bode well for Jennifer, and I didn't realize my selfishness until I listened to her hyperventilate as the tattooist disinfected the strip of spine where she was getting her Chinese character inked. Her boyfriend tried to soothe her with words and hand-holding, while I sat paralyzed with critiques of my own stupid idea for a tattoo. Even though I had lived with the phrase written by my bed, repetitively scrawled across my notebooks, and echoing through my mind for over a year of obsessing about wanting and being you, doubt possessed me. How could I trust anything I liked? How could I ever know who I was?

I couldn't back out now. What would that say to Jennifer, who'd been loyal to me since sixth grade when everyone and Thúy hated me, and to this guy with glasses who was breaking state laws AND giving me something for free? I was at least Asian enough to know not to pass up something free. I lay down on the couch and rolled down the waistband of my black jeans to bare the perma-paunch where I'd decided to get the tattoo. It was where I felt everything.

Constantly nauseated. Constantly constipated. I'd imbued this backwater tattoo with some potential power to heal me and all my chronic ailments.

"This part of the body tends to hurt a lot," he warned. I already knew.

His girlfriend leaned over the back of the couch, watching her boyfriend's hands clean off my stomach right above my pubic line. She stood up momentarily to roll down her own waistband and reveal a brushstroke style cat pawing at a butterfly that was just a couple of black ink whisps on her skin. They looked like the perfect wingtips of eyeliner drawn by the cholas I admired at school. My eyes could never hold eyeliner without lashes, smearing and smudging with every blink of skin against skin.

"Cute," I said. She nodded and returned to her hover.

Her boyfriend, perhaps shaky from her surveillance, had to redraw my letters three times. By the third draft, I could tell he was growing impatient with the amount of work he was doing for free. I didn't want to cause him any more trouble than what my exposed hipbones were clearly already stirring in his girlfriend, so I didn't correct the askew second line of text—an asymmetry that I knew would torment me.

That very night, the fresh needle wounds searing and itching Tennessee Williams' words across my stomach, I started to obsess. As we made out with Air Force men at a party that night, I tongued the inside of the fuel specialist's mouth in a rhythm with a symmetry that my tattoo needed. Later, in Jennifer's bathroom while she slept, I measured each tattooed letter with a ruler and mirror, the three-quarters and one-eighths of an inch in incongruities pounding out a soundtrack that swelled and faded, but never quieted, alongside every thought. The next day, my last day in Oklahoma, I pretended to be cool. Everyone in Altus already knew about my tattoo because everyone in Altus knew everything about everyone before they knew themselves, so, when prompted, I flashed the curled tails of letters peeking above the waist of my pants. When asked, I shrugged off the pain, then raised an eyebrow and bit my lower lip as I'd seen you do for countless photographers who'd unwittingly created my wallpaper. If anything but not myself, I had learned to be a good mimic. You gave me a mask for my throb of anxiety that made me hate everything I said, did, and was.

Back at my mother's house—the source—I was surprised to find a new comforter on my bed. The majority of her surprises were stomach-plummeting revelations of harbored resentment born out of

CHAPTER 15

fleeting moments and suicidal confessions. But the surprises that showed she thought of me with love were few and far between. There had been the ceramic E.T. coin bank, the glazed pastry shaped like the rotund pig that was my zodiac sign, and now this bed set in red and green and covered in vines.

I dropped my bags next to the freshly made bed (she had taken care to tuck the corners) and held onto the moment. Foolish from the tenderness of her gesture, I shared with her my tattoo, pulling up my shirt before I'd even finished saying cảm ơn for the comforter. The disappointment and disapproval dusked from her kohled eyebrows to her mouth, and my organs accordingly plummeted like a pelican into water. As was our symbiotic dance of emotional torture, my mother walked away without saying anything.

Her silence propelled me to scrape off, by fingernail and butterknife's edge, what I could of the still-scabbing inklines across my stomach. I laid out back-of-magazine laser tattoo removal ads beside my checkbook log, each line of numbers precisely inked, unlike those on my skin.

She refused to look at me, and the erasure increasingly thickened the air around me over the course of each day of her silent treatment. It was a buffer between us, but it also suffocated me. It squeezed my esophagus to the point that I could not swallow food or wear anything but a low V-neck shirt, which I worked into my you-obsessed wardrobe.

To redirect the pain, I plucked the few lashes I had left. I was grateful for one remaining thick root; when it broke the skin, the wet of its pulp sent a rippling ache up and down my body. I dragged this little white ball of wetness across my bald eyelid and my lips until it dried. Tracing my body with a piece of what had just been inside it was at least a delay between the next pluck, so I made it last as long as possible, rolling the lash between my thumb and forefinger before I blew it off and it was lost in the comforter's vines. I lay on the bed about to move to my thin eyebrows when she entered still without looking at me.

"Are you a gangster?"

I laughed. And then she said the phrase that always stopped me in my tracks: "In Việt Nam . . ." After a few cycles about tattoos as the marks of murderers and rapists and unemployable at jobs with health insurance and so pretty much already-dead, given the hepatitis that was passed down to me in our blood (with a sprinkling of Buddhist body-as-a-temple lecture ending with questions of how could I be buried with such an altered body), she paused. Nearly hyperventilating, I rambled back a response about Tennessee Williams and literature bringing me closer to God. Prayer. I did not mention you. My mother would not have been able to handle the news that I was a gangster *and* attracted to women.

She did not hear it. To do so would have required getting to know me.

Instead of following my plan to save up for the laser removal, I spent my retail paychecks on every magazine that featured you. I studied your tattoos and every word of your interviews about how you'd overcome self-harming behaviors and, later, how you dedicated yourself to saving children in countries fighting the never-ending aftermath of war. I invested in you, Angelina Jolie, to prove to me that I wasn't all the horrible things my own mother saw me as. If you were smart and beautiful and adored, then somewhere I could be more than deserving of already-deadness.

And, maybe, if I could collect enough, and if I had the tattoo to prove it, then maybe you could sense my love, my need. If I were anything like you, then perhaps you could sense that I was worthy of being saved too. Could you feel it? Maybe at any moment my telepathy would kick in and we would be bound. Maybe there was a magical power of connection in these magazines that I collected and bought special storage racks for—that is, until you adopted a little Vietnamese boy and renamed him Pax, or Peace. I stopped collecting you then. The saving had to end.

CHAPTER 16

THERAPIST 4

After another therapist, this one was the first I chose and went to by myself. She was Chinese American and the same age as my mother. She liked to tell me about the lunches she ordered from a new Chinese restaurant down the street. "Not bad," she shrugged. She also shared that her husband was white. Together, they had two daughters who looked completely different: one white, one Chinese.

"No, really?" I was fascinated. I didn't think that was possible. I had just assumed every Mỹ lai kid blended into unrecognizable—and easily denied—paternity as I had. My therapist pulled out two wallet-sized school photos. The elder daughter had a thin nose sprinkled with freckles and light eyes. She looked like an extra on a TGIF show. The younger sister had a round face and wide nose, and she lacked the infamous eyelid fold. I wondered if she hated her older sister.

Instead, I said, "Wow, they're beautiful. Like supermodels."

"Oh no," the therapist responded, and for a moment I was relieved that I didn't have a mother who was trained in thinking about emotions. "They are who they are."

"So tell me," she pivoted, "who are you?"

It was an impossible question for me to answer. I'd never been asked

CHAPTER 16

"who." It had always been "*what* are you?" If I had, I'm sure I wouldn't have been heard. I felt guilty and ashamed for everything that I was and like a failure for every person I'd tried to be to earn my parents' love, to gain a measure of acceptance from any and every Vietnamese person I'd ever met. It was also impossible to ask for help, even from a therapist, with figuring out who I was. In a previous session, I'd let it slip that I would feel relieved to be dead, just to escape my own thoughts. Her response was enough for me to resolve to keep it light, doable for her and for me.

"How is the CBT doing for the plucking?"

My hands adjusted the pillow I always placed over my stomach. "It's helping," I lied. "Thank you. The book, it's good."

"Do you mind," she asked, gesturing toward the couch where I was sitting. My throat tightened, but I nodded so as not to cause trouble. She sat down next to me, and when her thigh touched mine my skin bristled from knee to earlobes. I looked straight ahead at the watercolor of an English countryside (surely some kind of undercover Rorschach test) as she peered down her glasses at my eyelids. "Hmph," she concluded, "I see the patches."

She returned to her armchair. "It's not really noticeable until you're very close up. If you had darker or lighter lashes, it would be more apparent. You're lucky to have the coloring you do."

In the racist histories of mixed people touted for passing and of Asian-White folks being prized for their "exotic" beauty, I always felt like a disappointment for not resembling Olivia Munn (who is also an admitted eyelash puller but nobody cares because she's Olivia Munn). Now, though, my mixedness was enough to camouflage my trichotillomania.

INTERLUDE-INTRUSION

Stroke

    Stroke

        Stroke

           Stroke

                Stroke

Don't
WaitWaitWaitWaitWaitWaitWaitWaitWaitWaitWaitWaitWaitWait-WaitWaitWaitWaitWaitW—AcheAcheAcheAcheAcheAcheAcheAcheAcheAcheAcheAcheAcheAcheAcheAcheAcheA cheAcheAcheAche

INTERLUDE-INTRUSION

AcheAcheAcheAcheAcheAcheAcheAcheAcheAcheAcheAcheAch eAch eAcheAcheAcheAcheAcheAcheAcheAche Pluck

                        Pl
                        u
                        c
                        k
                        Pl
                        u
                        c
                        k
                        Pl
                        u
                        c
                        k

Re
Pla
y
Lo
ok
Mourn and Grieve
Look at yourself
Punish
Pu
Nis
h
Pu
Nis
h

CHAPTER 17

"UNDERCOVER GOOK"

During my teenaged every-other-weekend with my dad, he took me to the library. I worked my way through shelves of Hollywood starlets' biographies and memoirs. They were paginated proof that an unknown, unremarkable girl could someday be noticed and transform into an Ava Gardner or Hedy Lamarr or Dolores del Río, or at least someone loveable—if even by strangers—then maybe by my mother too. These life stories glamorized the rich twenties that were coming up for me. I assumed that they would be full and life-changing.

Now, on the other side of that decade, I have a very different story to tell. These were years of avoidance. I was hiding. As one of my acquaintances once told me, I was "an undercover gook." (Hold onto your pants, he was Vietnamese too. So, you know, it's okay.) Trudging through PhD programs in Cultural Studies and Literature, respectively, he and I joked about the stereotype of Vietnamese being more evasive than the orientalist inscrutable pan-Asian, what with the Việt Cộng's tunnels and jungle warfare. Plus, I was able to pass (maybe not as white, but as Mexican or Filipina). At a Tết

CHAPTER 17

party at one of our advisors' homes full of Vietnamese people, my friend told me, "You just pop up like boom, nổi tiếng Việt, and everybody like giật mình. I'm looking at you and listening to you.... Em, you an undercover gook."

I was undercover in the ways of romance, too. The Vietnameseness was easy enough to hide from my non-Vietnamese partners, more than one of whom reveled in my racial ambiguity: "I've never dated anyone who looked like you before." I was never able to get a Vietnamese man to date me because, they all said, "You're too much," laughing and shaking their heads, pre-shamed, "for my parents." The closest I got to them was scrolling through pictures of "gia đình" tattoos or rock-climbing, but mostly their ABGs-turned-wives leaning into cleavage framed by their manicured nails curling into a heart, their Vietnamese children smiling and jumping in the open. I wasn't too much. Just not enough.

The hairpulling was harder to hide. I turned down guys of a certain height—right in the 5'10" to 6'2" range—because the angle of our difference enunciated my lashlessness. One lapse in judgment resulted in a tall drink of water calling my lash-pulling "absurd." I consciously, obsessively, controlled the angles of my eyes to minimize the visibility of my patchy lashes. There was no doe-like flirtation by flapping my lashes. I had to either awkwardly look away or directly at them. The latter was hard for me because I registered each of their most minor facial expressions as an impending rejection. It was sensory overload to simply look at my partners' faces. As a twenty-something-year-old me would, I often distracted potential partners from my abused lashes and brows with cleavage-baring V-necks, which also conveniently helped the choking feeling in my throat.

And when I did stumble into a relationship, it never lasted more than a few months. Many of these partners were already in love with other people, which they never admitted, so usually the relationship ended because of things that would hone my skill in turning pain into laughter. One guy confessed on our first date that he liked Mexican chicas best, and I silently bit into my taco as he asked me on a second date to escort him to the doctor. Another announced that his bucket list included to date an Asian girl (#2) and to date a white girl (#14). His friend hitchhiked his thumb at me and asked, "Isn't she the best of both worlds?" He crinkled his nose and scoffed,

"No." Another guy's mother literally stirred mayonnaise into potato salad as she told me, "You're not really Vietnamese, though. Not really." I felt like I'd been donkey-kicked in the chest. "So why do you say that?" she asked. "For attention?"

Other times, relationships ended abruptly because I stressed about disclosing my liver disease to them. Though I contracted it through birth from a homeland where it was endemic, Pamela Anderson had made everyone think that hepatitis was purely sexually transmitted. But it was not sexy. "You're so hot," grinding, and then, "Are you up to date on your immunizations?"

Other times, I broke it off just to avoid getting too close. I ran away a lot. The Columbian surfer I had started dating while in Black Studies 100 had a little sister I bonded with and whose mother I loved because, even though she was perplexed that I didn't eat the copious amounts of beef and chorizo she cooked daily, she hugged me and talked to me in the maternal ways I craved. A few months in, I got sucked into a bout of depression and anxiety that resulted in a completely bald right eyelid. The asymmetry with my left eye's lashes unsettled me, made me antsy. I didn't want to do it, but I began to pluck, like work, the left lashes down to thin patches to balance out the asymmetry. When my boyfriend came to visit, I still couldn't break out of the shame paralysis enough to even change out of pajamas, though I did scrawl sloppy black lines over my bald eyelids, as if it helped. I knew that he would notice and it would be yet another "I'm sick" talk that we would need to have. So that day, I sat with him on the front porch of my mother's house so that she wouldn't eavesdrop on every word and use it against me later, and I broke up with him so that I could avoid having the eyelash conversation. I could just regrow alone. When he left, he said, "My mom said she knew you never loved me." Yet another mother secretly harboring hatred for me was enough to send me back to my bed with a compact mirror and tweezers to watch the punishment I was to inflict on the few remaining lashes of my left eye.

A few years later, I started my first graduate degree (the big moneymaker of an MFA in Creative Writing). Even though I was the first in my family to get this far in my education, it all happened quietly, invisibly. I didn't walk in the graduation ceremony for my bachelor's degree because I was

CHAPTER 17

still hurting from the fact that my mom hadn't attended my high school graduation because the weather was "too hot." My BA diploma arrived in the mail, and I kept it in its "Do Not Bend" mailer and slipped it into my bookcase. Just as quietly, I began my master's. As much as I hoped that these educational accomplishments would change our relationship, my mother did not ask anything about my schooling.

At the time, she was obsessed with Farmville, the Facebook game in which you could dabble in genetic engineering through an avatar in overalls who cultivated crops and raised a menagerie of animals. My mother's "farm" dominated her attention. She hadn't worked in over a decade, no longer had hobbies or friends, and was marginal to my now-teenaged siblings' independent routines of school, sports, and the extracurricular activities of American kids. All of her intense energy funneled into Farmville. The symmetry of her crop lines was impeccable. Her animals were fat and smiling in the pens she had built for them. The farm was decorated with ten of everything that the game offered as rewards—outhouses, lampposts, grandfather clocks, fountains. It was an outdoor hoarders' paradise. Where failure gaped wide, Farmville was my mother's digital filling up.

While I worked early and late hours in an austere office on my coursework, master's thesis manuscript, and TAing for the university's composition courses, Farmville notifications pinged on my computer. They were requests from my mother to send her seeds or congratulate her on her harvest. Then she would text to remind me to check my farm to earn rewards that she thought would look good on my plot of land. It was all pretend. But she was relentless. My siblings deleted the game out of exhaustion from the persistence of her requests. I kept going. It was something we were accomplishing together.

Halfway through my master's program, I found lê thị diễm thúy's *The Gangster We Are All Looking For* (at a bookstore in the mall, she adds oldly). The world within me broke open. It was the first time that I'd read a book from, about, for Vietnamese Americans. I felt seen and heard and assured that I was—we were—real. Up until then, I had only read literature about Việt Nam through the cringey adjectives of Robert Olen Butler's *A Good Scent from a Strange Mountain*, which I read because, as an English major,

I was trained to believe that I had something important to learn from white men writing about Việt Nam. One of my creative writing teachers assigned us Graham Greene's *The Quiet American*. I admitted to my professor that I could not read past the first chapter in which Phuong is introduced as "fragile as a bird." Still, he pointedly asked me, "What do you think about Greene's portrayal of the Vietnamese woman? Why does she act this way? Is it culturally accurate?" I inhaled as deeply as Greene's opium-toking narrator.

With lê's *Gangster*, for the first time, what I was living connected with what I was reading and what I could be writing. My thesis manuscript was razed. Re-seeded.

"Mẹ," I reached out one day, "I read a book about a girl from Việt Nam." She was cooking or washing dishes or something; all I remember was that she was not looking at me and was silent so I wasn't sure if she was listening to what I was saying. But I was so excited about lê's novel that I ventured further, risking rebuke for what I thought could be the connection between me, my mother, and writing. "Her brother died, but when she comes here, he's still with her. The water—"

She sucked her teeth. She'd been listening to everything I said. Two of her brothers, my uncles, had died. "I live that. Why I need to read?"

I would eventually get her attention when I started dating a mixed Japanese American man. My mom grew like an inflatable tube man and her eyes widened. "Oooh, người Nhật. The *rich* Asian!" She had no shame in trying to climb this colorist ladder that left what Ali Wong called us "jungle Asians" swinging from the bottom rung. "What his name? Suzuki? Honda? Nintendo?"

"Yep, Mẹ. I'm dating Johnny Nintendo."

"I don' know!" She cracked up without covering her teeth with her hand as she usually did. She was just giddy about the incoming palettes of Shiseido skin-lightening creams. "Good not Mitsubishi. Sound like 'itchy pussy.'"

"Wow, Mẹ ơi, your wedding toast is writing itself," but she couldn't hear me. She was giggling about money and sushi.

Counter to my mother's wishes that I be beautiful and rich, the thousands of pages of grad school reading strained my eyes to necessitate glasses.

CHAPTER 17

New anxieties grew around the optometrist's comments and questions: "Em, being lai is so lucky. Hazel eyes are very rare. Not boring brown like the rest of us." Then a pause as I choked on my guilt and she zoomed in with her lighted lens. "What happened to your eyelashes?" I first tried to lie that they fell out on their own. Midway through her cautionary lecture on how hair loss could be a symptom of a much deeper health issue, I confessed that I had pulled them out. "Oh," she said, "well lashes protect your eyes from dirt, mites . . ." I disappeared from myself right about then, overwhelmed by literally being so visible. I wanted to be seen, but not like this.

Once I was officially a stereotypical bespectacled English major, I was grateful for the barrier between my lashless eyes and anyone looking at me, and the tortoiseshell frames lent some definition to my nearly browless fivehead. The problem, though, was how I stupidly winced every time my nails clicked against the lenses when my hand instinctually reached for my lashes while I was reading, struggling to sleep, planning any activity, balancing my checkbook, getting into my car, getting out of my car, looking at myself in the mirror, avoiding looking at myself in the mirror, and waking up heavied by another day.

Glasses-blocked, I shifted to pulling out the hair from my head. I remember the moment I shifted. While sitting in bed reading onion skin–thin pages of shell-shocked British soldiers' poetry from what they saw as the first World War, I ran my fingers through my hair and zeroed in on a hair whose root pinched even from the casual swipe. I parted the other hairs to isolate this one painful root. I tugged at it and felt the sweet ache of a wet root like that of my former lashes. The sensation made me salivate. My legs ached as if they needed to burst into a run. I wound the hair around my finger and let my hand fall dead. The weight ripped out an oblong wet root, three times the length of my lash roots. My body buzzed. I rubbed the moist root along the creases in my lips, which I had to rub when they started to tickle. Once the root began to air dry, I pinched it with the thumb and forefinger of my opposite hand, pressing the nails together to scrape the root off of the hair and into a minuscule white ball. It disappeared. The rest of the hair didn't interest me, so I shook it off my hand. It floated onto my outstretched legs and felt as unnerving as cobwebs. I quickly brushed it off. I was only interested in the roots. I began searching my head for other hairs that promised the pain of ejecting a fat wet root.

It was exciting that there was so much more head hair than lashes, and I found that the level of pain varied according to the part of the head. The crown had more of a deep ache than the superficial yet eye-watering pinches at my temples and back of the neck. In particular, most satisfying were the hairs along my middle part that I'd had since childhood and at the back right bend of my crown where my Dennis the Menace cowlick was. The different angle my body had to hold to rip out my head hair turned into shoulder and neck pain, then migraines, which I just attributed to a reader's life. As I pulled, I scanned hundreds of pages of British and American literature, as well as squinted at the dwindling numbers in my bank account that had me eating Top Ramen and canned beans each night. Every degree I pursued increased my stress and thus my hairpulling; every opportunity and success rolled into more punitive self-loathing.

I pulled peacefully and gently while losing myself in Jean Rhys's *Wide Sargasso Sea* and everything Herman Melville wrote.

I angry-fisted chunks of hair out after the professor of my Virginia Woolf seminar (my favorite course) asked, in front of the whole class, "Did you write this paper yourself, Jude? It's just so compelling." This white British (double whammy!) professor's microaggression was ironic because he had also been the first professor to recommend that I pursue writing in graduate school and as a career. It became a trend that the people who pigeonholed me also pushed me along, and so my sense of indebtedness grew with the smaller they made me feel.

> *"And then, letting her eyes slide imperceptibly above the pool and rest on that wavering line of sea and sky, on the tree trunks which the smoke of steamers made waver upon the horizon, she became with all that power sweeping savagely in and inevitably withdrawing, hypnotised, and the two senses of that vastness and this tininess (the pool had diminished again) flowering within it made her feel that she was bound hand and foot and unable to move by the intensity of feelings which reduced her own body, her own life, and the lives of*

CHAPTER 17

all the people in the world, for ever, to nothingness. So listening to the waves, crouching over the pool, she brooded" (Woolf 75–76).

As microaggressions often snowball, my part widened after a creative writing professor started a workshop about my story, inspired by lê, set in Việt Nam, with, "You've invented a whole new world." I wanted to say, "It's Việt Nam. It's not new. It exists." But I didn't. I remained silent as some of my classmates perpetuated the professor's tone by piling on with more Orientalist commentary and questions:

"Aren't Asians supposed to be close with their elders?"

"How is she so articulate if she's speaking in Vietnamese?"

"How does she make money if she's just dancing at a bar all night?"

"Why would her children all look different? How is that possible?"

Though I found friends and writers in the MFA program who continue to inspire me to this day, these others' comments still haunt me. Researchers do say that bad memories stick with us more in order to help us survive. So, in a way, I'm grateful to these ghosts for guiding me to stop writing fiction and, instead, keeping me alive by writing my truths, even when they were hard to say out loud.

On one of the dates early in our relationship, Johnny Nintendo and I sat under a hanging lamp at a restaurant. We shared tacos and fries while talking about books and writing. Suddenly, he interrupted my deliriously nervous laugh with his own laughter. "I'm sorry," he said. "It's just that, you're sitting under this light and it's shining on the giant part you have in your hair. Why is it so wide?"

Despite (or maybe because of) my silences, my amygdala can be fucking fire. I have slammed my palms on a shitty driver's hood and yelled until they rolled up the window that I was ready to yank her through. I have half-tackled a bitch in clear platform heels because I could not take another white girl edging me off the sidewalk because she thinks her privilege earns her the right-of-way over women of color, over women whose hair is not as long or lush or as floral-scented as hers.

But because that very same amygdala has been wounded it also shrinks into plankton-small submission, especially in situations with men. And always in everything having to do with my hair.

It was early in the relationship, and I was determined to make a relationship last for more than a few months. I needed to prove that I was tolerable, if not loveable. My mother had proven to me that I was difficult to love, if at all, so if only I could make it to four months.... Even though talking about my thinning hair was enough to make me want to flee in embarrassment and shame, I was determined not to do that here. I was almost twenty-five: the age my mother had always told me was the goal for being married with a house and her grandchildren on the way. A firstborn daughter's duty. So I stayed in that unflatteringly lit booth.

"Uh, yeah, I guess I need some more protein," and with this classy semen joke I would have winked but I couldn't show my thinned lashes, so I flipped my hair to the side and desperately inhaled tortilla chips and salsa while he talked about things that I told myself I had to care too much about in order to make him stay. Now that he had noticed my hair problem, I had to work harder to prove that I was worthwhile, to earn his partnership.

When he asked me to wear headbands and scarves to all of his family functions and get-togethers with friends, I of course agreed. "I don't want them to think that you have cancer or something. I don't want them to worry."

"What if they ask? Can't I just tell them?"

"That would be weird."

I did not want to cause problems, especially to a welcoming and loving family whose sweet matriarch had survived internment. I did not want to be the burden that I felt I was to my mother and family who'd already suffered so much. I mimicked Bà Ngoài's strategic bobby-pinning to keep in place the head scarves that I altered my wardrobe to coordinate with. Floral headbands didn't exactly match with oversized Ramones shirts and pajama pants.

For Shōgatsu, or Japanese New Year, Johnny and I attended the celebration at his family's Shinto church where they practiced the centuries-old ritual of mochitsuki: pounding rice into mochi with a wooden mallet. Feeling like I was at temple on my period again, I tried to stay invisible on the periphery of the circle of family and community members watching Johnny and his brothers and cousins take turns in the tandem dance of

CHAPTER 17

sprinkling the rice with water and then pounding it with the massive mallet. The grains of rice began to melt into each other, creating a soft pillow of mochi. They were all together in this. They were all here in the moment, not pained by the past or worried about a future that might not be there. At the same time, this moment felt so much bigger than itself, as it was connected to the ancestors and traditions that came before. It was moving. I began to tear up but held back, as is my superhero power, to avoid smearing the eyeliner that filled in the bald spots on my eyelids.

Then, they called me to the mallet and usu. Though they did it out of love and invitation to belong to this circle of time and tradition, it felt to me like a call to ritual sacrifice. Like the mochi would mushroom into a giant demon and boom, "Balding Vietnamese girl! You will be our petty offering to the all-powerful gods of Clan Nintendo!"

I didn't want to. I wanted to disappear back into my comfortable invisibility half-crying the day away from afar. But I also remembered that I needed to work harder than others. I was a jungle Asian with visible symptoms of mental illness. I had to earn being in the company of the Japanese rung of the ladder we'd built.

My hands were strong from pulling hair every day. It takes a lot of muscle tension and control to pluck for extended periods of time. But I did not have strength in the rest of my arm. I was missing it from the sports my mother prohibited me from playing. The Nintendos had all been athletes in multiple sports and could suspend themselves horizontally on stop sign poles, so I tried to politely decline, even though I know it came off as rude and I was more sorry than I could say. I longed to feel a part of something much bigger than my own loud mind hating itself. I was moved to welling tears as I watched the cousins pound mochi in concert. I started to smile.

Then my headband slipped.

Johnny caught me by the elbow and leaned in to say, "I can see a thinning spot on the back of your head." He was reminding me of the one thing I already could never allow myself to forget.

I had created for myself a condition that forced me to lie and hide in ways that I hated witnessing and being taught to emulate. It was no coincidence that, from Johnny on, I would date a string of people who kept me a secret. I was communicating to all my partners, with every furtive blink and unspoken urge, that I deserved to be hidden, that I was worthy of my invisibility. In the absence of hair, that was what grew.

CHAPTER 18

HOT DOGS

By the time I entered a PhD program in literature, I was ripping the hair from my scalp while writing every grad school assignment under the cloud of imposter syndrome and during equally regular arguments with my boyfriends who, more than once, told me that I made them want to kill themselves. I was a spreading disease. Visibility was vengeance. Becoming a doctor (even though not a "real" doctor) convinced everyone that I was thriving, but every semester of straight A's made me more desperate for someone to notice my increased hairpulling as a sign that I, despite being high-functioning, was suffering.

The ponytails that I loved so much because they reminded me of my mother's touch were now thin like the extra fabric shredded on a tailor's floor. No matter how much I brushed and bobby-pinned my hair, it was lumpy because of the bald spots widening underneath what was becoming a comb-over. Each hair depended on the other. At the orientation for the doctoral program, an ocean breeze lifted my comb-over, and I watched my new cohort members' eyes linger on my head. I swallowed into my closing throat and tried to keep making them laugh as a distraction. "PhD? Stand for Phuc-ing Douchebag, huh?" I said, impersonating a Vietnamese accent. It always got a laugh.

CHAPTER 18

The PhD program was the first time I had an Asian American teacher since Ms. Ono. Many of my fellow students were also people of color. But this was far from a liberation movement. In line with the university's corporate practices, the parking permits were so egregiously expensive that I parked a mile and a half off campus and hauled a backpack full of books back and forth at all hours of long study and work days. The weight on my shoulders exacerbated the aches and pains that hairpulling caused in my hands, arms, shoulders, neck, and head. Migraines seared, and nerves began pinching from behind my right eye all the way down my back and into my legs. The half-moon callouses on my hairpulling fingers grew so coarse and thick that they began to sluff off, along with newly developed eczema scales on those two fingers.

The literature building that I walked to was literally killing people; as a result of a chemical leak that had been investigated and then covered up, double digits of faculty and staff had become chronically ill or died from various cancers. The department chair that welcomed me to the program was dead before I graduated. When we returned from one winter recess, we found the top floor of classrooms coated in black mold, but the college claimed there weren't funds to raze and rebuild. Through the window of a classroom in which I studied vampire literatures, I watched cranes erect a brand-new metal and glass cathedral to Engineering, one of the Department of Defense–funded moneymakers on campus. I began meeting my cancer-fearing professors at the coffee shop or in windy courtyards just to avoid our building. We were literally a dying breed.

To be fair, my tuition was covered as long as I worked as a TA for professors who didn't care about their students. "They have no common sense," one professor vented to me as he sighed leaving the classroom. The professors read or recited their own esoteric scholarship to darkened lecture halls of undergraduates watching soccer games on their laptops or sharing headphones and passing pinkeye. What kept me awake during one of these most boring of courses was tallying the number of times he said "Right?" at the end of every statement, even if it was factual—the epitome of academia's empty discourse. The onus of *actually* teaching the material fell on the shoulders of underpaid TAs like me who had to transform the lecture content into engaging educational activities and guide students through doing the assignments themselves rather than the systemic norm of paying someone else to do it.

Since I was already teaching at local community colleges (my mom taught me to always have a side hustle), I was experienced at turning what students saw as boring material into short-form entertainment. It was the least I could do for those who were suffering the burnout and cynicism of the professors they (or their parents) were paying top dollar for. But it helped me too. The classroom was the stage on which I got to spotlight the codeswitching I'd been doing my whole life. The more I taught, the more I heard, "Your class is so fun," and, the most memorable in its multiplicity, "You should be a stand-up comedian." Even though my gaping bald spots dashed my and my mother's hopes for fame (I could no longer even soothe myself with eye-clenched concentration on red carpet fantasies), at least I could perform as a teacher. I could give students a break from their boring classes and give myself a break from my relentless thoughts hellbent on killing me. "You're so different in front of people," one of my partners told me during this time. Perfect.

My supervisors regularly observed my classes and, with years of teaching experience at other colleges, I always received positive feedback. Except when one administrator ended his evaluation of me with, "Before you leave, one thing to work on is your accent. E-nun-ci-ate so that you don't send our students the wrong idea. Low-class slang might sound 'cool,' but it is not correct English." Pluck. Pull. Rip.

Despite the protective armor that teaching was helping me cement, it was in these R1 university classrooms that mostly young white male students wore me the fuck down. One "anonymous" student evaluation (and, come on, we all know who it is, even if their name is not on it) wrote, "She distracts me from learning with THAT BODY." A different branch of the same tree had other birds cawing that I did not know what I was talking about and that their fathers had taught them differently (read: "the Truth"), and they were constantly challenging the grades I assigned. In an Asian American literature class, I shared the news about Mark Wahlberg acknowledging his Marky Mark–era hate crime against elderly Vietnamese

CHAPTER 18

men that left one of them blind. I shared that I wouldn't pay any amount of money to watch films or buy products endorsed by someone who had committed an act of hate. A young white male started a tirade.

"That's so stupid! The person he is in life is separate from who he is in the movies and—"

"Okay, but if I pay to see the person he is in movies, that benefits the actor who blinded an old Vietnamese man and now has more money to make that all go away. And his movies are shitty anyway."

"But—"

A Chinese American student, buff and tatted, interjected: "Show her some respect and shut the fuck up."

As soon as that interjection had restored my faith in humanity and my Asian American pride, a student who was a veteran of the Israeli military asked me to help her write an article for the school newspaper. Just a "little op-ed," she claimed, arguing against the campus protests in support of divestment, condemning Palestinian "terrorists," and advocating for continued genocide. "Will you help me spread this important message?" she asked. Teaching took advantage of my tendency to say yes to my mother, to everyone I felt I needed to earn acceptance (if not love) from, so that traumatized part of me struggled not to say yes to help a student, regardless of where she came from. Saying no was a scary defining of self and setting of boundaries. I bit my lip from launching into continuities of colonialism and genocide, and how we should know better than most what it does to reduce people to numbers from an aerial lens, and an Angela Davis quote I was struggling to remember about how "our histories never unfold in isolation." I felt like I couldn't escape colonialism, not even in an education system that I thought promised to liberate and empower, and the anger-anxiety-fear it fostered in me twinned my trauma. I hid my trembling hands under the desk as I racked my brain for a diplomatic way to say, "No."

One of her classmates chimed in. "War is crazy," he said. I was hopeful that I wouldn't have to regulate alone. He looked straight at me. "It's crazy that my grandfather fought against your people. And now we're sitting in the same room." I limited my response to a quick explanation about North and South Việt Nam. Later, and still sometimes today, I replayed the interaction and all the things I did and did not say. Replay and rip.

These were the students who would be designing and operating the DOD-funded drones that were tested over campus every day. And these would be the drones that would be the US's aerial optics over people like my Vietnamese family members. Tug tug until unbearable, then rip.

In one seminar, we discussed a text about US-perpetrated wars in Asia over the past century, and a line referred to the innocent victims of bombings. A fellow student—also Asian American—hooked and swiveled her finger near her chin, which was her erudite way of raising her hand. "What is 'innocent' anyway?" she posed. "Can we interrogate this rhetoric?" Seething, I stormed out of the classroom and into the night with test drones humming above. Here we were, so many of us fighting to be the first in our families to achieve this level of privilege, and we were wasting it—insulting it—by moralizing our people who had been murdered by the military-industrial complex. I thought of my grandmother, my mother, all my uncles and cousins who fled bombs all for this PhD student to "interrogate the rhetoric of their innocence." And I was complicit in it by virtue of internalizing insecurities about my "low-class" accent, too afraid to speak back to the hateful posturing of another student with seemingly more sophisticated finger gestures. Select and tweeze.

Being around the supposedly most educated people I'd ever been around only sharpened focus on the fact that I was a mixed Vietnamese American woman. I was an extension of the histories of oppression I was researching in my people's literature. Same shit, different setting. Though I bonded with two other women—one a Palestinian and the other a Chicana—who understood the way our bodies revolted against ourselves, I ultimately retreated into myself and the past. I spent nights and weekends reading about the atrocities during the US war in Việt Nam and the myriad struggles Vietnamese experienced while becoming "American." I cannot list the most resounding information I exhumed in my research.

Because it wasn't just research. Theory was not just a "tool to think through," as my cohort members annoyingly repeated. Everything I was reading and writing became a way to smooth the puzzle of what I was living.

CHAPTER 18

This came to a head as I was writing a dissertation chapter on mixed-race Vietnamese children, starting with the war. As part of my "research," I invited my youngest auntie (also mixed) to a screening of Tammy Lee Nguyen's documentary, *Operation Babylift: The Lost Children of Vietnam*. We listened to the adoptees cry through their-our struggles in the shadow of the American GI–Vietnamese prostitute narrative and the resounding echo of "What are you?": racism, violence, isolation, untraceable health problems, survivor's guilt, and, of course, suicide.

Then I went back further, magnetically pulled to Việt Nam. I analyzed the allegorical poem, *The Tale of Kieu*, that elegizes the eponymous Vietnamese girl's descent into prostitution and victimization by invading foreigners, the resulting mixed children elided from the narrative altogether. To center the mixed child, I drew into conversation Kien Nguyen's *The Unwanted: A Memoir of Childhood*, which at the time was the only text I knew written by a mixed Vietnamese person. It was all so fucking awful. I could see and feel and remember the shame of being a half-breed whose life sprung from a war that killed over three million of our people. I had to confront that if I was born that .5 of a generation earlier I would have been walking evidence of what Foucault (a PhD program is pure dunktanking in Foucault) named biopolitics and what Giorgio Agamben sharpened in his theory-not-a-theory of those in the "state of exception." Agamben wrote that those others are "life that does not deserve to live." As mixed children of Việt Nam, we were "bare life," worthy of death or always-already dead. Fuck.

At the same time, the Việt Nam half of Nguyen's memoir tremored on the mournful croon of cải lương that my grandma and mom listened to, swaying or rocking, on Sundays after morning cleaning. Dripping with all the embodied tragedy, it felt like we were justifying the response of people who, when they found out we were Vietnamese, tilted their head the way you might if you came across a disabled dog and responded, "awwww." The US half of Nguyen's autobiographical story was worse, all gratitude and dentistry and model minority happy happy joy joy (that's right, that's a *Ren & Stimpy* reference because I want you to feel as gross as I felt). A straight upward line, just like Freytag's arc that Greene-loving creative writing teachers had instructed me was the way a good story should be told, the way America kept telling me a good life should be lived.

Learning about our history and my bare life deepened my depression to the point that I dug through old pictures to send to the family and friends who I thought would keep them after I killed myself. I wrote the letters. I planned on pills but fantasized about a gunshot to the temple. Pull, pull, pull. The part in my hair widened, bare.

Nevertheless, I kept completing the rigorous workload for the program. In fact, it was during this time that I fine-tuned my system of checklists and Post-its—a CSI-type web of fragments that kept me constantly working to connect, to complete another puzzle. When I felt like drowning, I cry-danced to Nicki Minaj's "Super Bass" and sang along with T.I.'s promises of "the old me dead and gone away." I binged *RuPaul's Drag Race* and tried—and failed—to replicate the artistic contouring that I hoped would shrink my nose and distract from my barely there lashes, brows, and hair. I learned how fucking miserable it is to sob while trying to swallow burritos at 2 a.m. And I just kept pulling and pushing, with the echoes of my dad's saying, "You can sleep when you're dead."

The only thing that buoyed me was writing blog posts for diaCRITICS, a website of the Diasporic Vietnamese Artists Network. The fact that I was invited to write by Viet Thanh Nguyen made me feel, for once, included. I was able to meet Vietnamese American authors like Bao Phi, GB Tran, and, yes, lê thị diễm thúy herself who had changed the course of my reading-writing-living. I felt less alone and a part, however small, of an important movement. Now that works by Vietnamese Americans were starting to be published, I read every single one, relishing the parallels and the diversities—most of all, the writers who shared how their mothers required them to pull their gray hairs too. The understanding made me want to pour out. diaCRITICS gifted me the opportunity to write creatively, which was a much-needed respite from the grind of academia's multisyllabic words and paragraph-long sentences to explain, essentially, a feeling. The late nights I spent piecing together diaCRITICS blogs like a puzzle of stories, pictures, interviews, and excerpts were great relief. Satisfying reprieve from pulling.

CHAPTER 18

It was this opportunity to express, belong, and receive validation that readied me for the most unexpected life-changing impact of being a diacritic. In my post reviewing Lily Hoang's brilliant *Changing*, I opened with the embarrassing confession that I had, as a child, vowed to marry Prince Eric from Disney's *The Little Mermaid*. When I sent out the link to this diaCRITICS post to friends and family, my divulged love for the red-sashed pretty boy of a sailor—animated, to boot—caught the attention (and laughter) of an old friend I'd met in the MFA program. Early in our workshops, he had written a short story, "Yoshimi and the Robot," that struck an emotional chord vibrating beyond the sci-fi setting. "Dawn" the robot signed in ASL to young Yoshimi, and internally I fell to my knees with the pain and beauty of it all. It had been from that line that I knew I had found someone who felt life in the same ways, ones that I could not yet articulate but I could look to him to show me.

At the time we were tied to others, so I admired him from afar in friendship. His workshop comments made me a better writer, and his jokes made me laugh harder than anyone I'd ever met. We remained casual friends when I moved away to the doctoral program, but this diaCRITICS post shrunk the distance. We were both newly single. I thought I would never consider dating a friend because my mother had always named her boyfriends as "just friends," so that had soured the whole idea for me. Yet, from our first date walking off gorgonzola fries at the ocean boardwalk in front of the Sons of Norway house, he made me feel seen and chosen in a way I had never known but always longed for. It was not until Mike that I knew what it was like to choose living because of, and for, love. He even liked my thin, uneven eyebrows. My sparse hair did not faze him. He saw me as, and made me feel, beautiful as myself. I do not believe anyone can solely save someone else from depression and suicidal thoughts, but I know that the transition from alone to together was life-saving for me. With him, I had a future and a life to build. I could see our yet-to-be-born children's hair blowing in breezes.

I needed to get out of the doctoral program. I could not quit because that would just give everyone who doubted me more ammunition; one step-uncle said, "Wow, PhD?! I thought you just smoke drug and homeless. Never doctor!" Instead, I needed to whittle down the six-year normative time. One thing I owe to a childhood of neglect and criticism is a ninja-caliber resting bitch face and refusal to kiss ass, which so many of the other students seemed to do. I wouldn't brown-nose, so I did what I do best: become invisible. On my own, I drafted enough of my dissertation so that my committee had no choice but to advance my candidacy. My growing depression and anxiety kept me inside enough hours to power through the workload. That was not the problem.

The only hurdle between me and graduating with a PhD in my fourth year was the language requirement. It would be easy to check off this box with French because I had minored in it during my undergraduate study. During my doctoral research, French had enabled me to read the extremely fucked racist rhetoric in original colonial documents about Việt Nam. (Smaller brains? Allez vous faire foutre, anthropologists!) But I wanted—needed—to decolonize by applying to the college's unique Vietnamese heritage language program. It aligned with my life and my dissertation (which *was* my life at that time), and I hoped that relearning my first language in a formal educational setting would give me other associations than the pain I felt with hearing my mother's voice.

I sat waiting in the university hallway for the esteemed Vietnamese language professor whose name had been lauded to my ears by many voices. I was overwhelmingly nervous but also excited to meet the person who could reconnect me to my language and culture, as well as ultimately stand in for my mother who, since I'd moved to the PhD program, had visited just once and called a few times only to confess her own latest bout of suicidal thoughts. I'd counseled her through and, in sync, my ideations sharpened.

"Hello, Professor," I said, scrambling to my feet and reaching for her hand. I'd been in the institution too long. She shook her head because, I assumed, I forgot to bow and call her Cô instead of Professor. Upon introduction alone, I was already losing points that I needed to be accepted into the exclusive and impacted Vietnamese program—a language requirement that I needed to graduate. Plucking ammunition was stockpiling.

In her office, she set down her hot dog in its paper boat that prevented ketchup from overflowing onto the framed picture of her white husband and a mixed son who belonged to one more place than I did. Up until

CHAPTER 18

that point, I had associated hot dogs with my dad's Angels baseball games that were long and nauseating because we were always losing. So we filled ourselves, and clapped and did the wave with mustard-crusted nails. She slid the hot dog into her mouth, chewing and spraying, and said to me, "Americans take Vietnamese culture. Are you doing the same?" Once again, my mixed face triggered pained aggression. In my guilt, I buried my disgust and complied with everything that this auntie asked of me. For the length of her tubed meat lunch, she hamster-cheeked chunks of bun to move her tongue around our language's dipthongs, tripthongs, tones, and dialects, chewing up home.

On a white sheet of paper she tossed me, I tried to prove to her I was not a hot dog thief. I scratched the words I knew with diacritical maps for a voice to find my meaning. When I filled the page, the hot dog filled her 'o' of surprise. She promised a place for me in her program for children born to scattered seeds and, as I moved toward the door, reached to embrace me. "Con," her mustard-scented voice called to my back in the way that a stadium anthem fades. Empty seats. Losing toward a new team.

I took a French seminar on Zola instead.

I did not walk in my graduation ceremony to be hooded. My doctoral diploma arrived at the end of my fourth year and remained unopened in its envelope on my bookshelf for eight years after that.

CHAPTER 19

DIEM, THE TAILOR

As I finished my doctorate, my grandmother began to die. Dementia crept in at sunset. "Your father and me," she'd tell me at twilight in the hospice, "we go ăn chả giò and uống bia." My grandmother had not seen my father in well over a decade, nor had they ever nhậu together with eggrolls and beer. She was not in any condition to go out, physically or mentally.

And it was her utmost concern that she did not look ready. She wasn't allowed to use her perfumes or makeup, save for the polish my aunties painted her nails with. Her hair had grown out the dye, so it was, for the first time I'd seen, white. It was still crispy from all the years of dyeing and perming. It looked, too, like tufts had fallen out, leaving Bà Ngoại's prided head of hair patchy. It looked like she was dying.

After every visit to her care facility, I winced only at the frustration with the *lack* of pain when I pulled both my thin, brittle lashes and the now coarse and uneven hair on my head and whatever few stubs persisted on my legs. My hairs' differences only compelled me more aggressively to

CHAPTER 19

continue plucking. There would never be enough hair for me to not look like Robert De Niro's scarred-til-smooth portrayal of Frankenstein's monster. I deserved it, though. I had missed out on so much time with my grandmother because I had given in to my mother's cautionary tales about her and then had wasted even more time in academia. This is what I was creating as my bà ngoại was dying.

Always kinder to others than I could be to myself, I told her I thought her hair looked lovely, like a bird's nest, in winter. I learned from my bà ngoại to hate bullshit compliments, so I don't know why I thought she would fall for that. She just adjusted her baseball cap, plain black without logos, like a bank robber. I helped her keep her hat straight when she mumbled herself into a sitting sleep or rolled over to adjust her IVs.

Despite her haze, it was with clear eyes and certain voice that she instructed me to get married in a green and yellow áo dài. "That would look best on you," she told me in Vietnamese. I did not ask questions. She was the kind of person who always hung up the phone before saying good-bye.

We left it at that, decided, and shortly thereafter she was released to go home where she died in the middle of the night, facedown and purpled.

I received my aunt's text message about Bà Ngoại's death while sitting in the dining room of the house that Mike and I had recently started living in together as fiancés. He found me collapsed and sobbing on our dinner table.

During the American part of her funeral, my youngest uncle played a slideshow of photographs he'd compiled from the decades that Bà Ngoại had loved posing for the camera. "Of all the grandchildren," he told me, "you had the most pictures with her." I could not see them clearly on the screen because I was crying so hard. I knew that the pictures lied. I had not spent the most time with her. Even the time I did have with her was through walls my mother's stories had built for me: *Don't trust her. Don't take her money; you'll owe her. Don't let her touch your hair if you don't want to be cursed. Don't believe her lies about me. Don't.* But everything inside me broke when my mother threw her body across the coffin, pounding and wailing "No" and "Mom-Má."

The home Mike and I now shared had a story. A WWII veteran had built the house himself after returning from service. He and his wife, both devout Catholics, raised their children there. It was their home for over fifty years. He had passed, but his wife was still alive in an assisted living facility. We were the only people to live in the house after them.

The nightmares started soon after I moved in. A man yelling at me, "You don't belong here." Chasing me down the hallway. "Get out!" Ripping the jade Phật Bà pendant from my neck.

Sure enough, in waking hours, the metal clasps holding Phật Bà to my chest began to bend and break, even after replaced once, twice. I nestled her into a velvety ring box on the altar I had set up to protect our home, not realizing that the threat would come from inside. Without Phật Bà to guard me, I nudged Mike every time I was awakened by a scream catching in my throat. He walked me to and from the bathroom, shielding me from the heavy hallway feeling that reminded me of my grandparents' house in Pedro.

When he was at work and I was alone in the house, I blasted the TV and walked from room to room with my back against the walls. I prayed for my bà ngoại's spirit to visit me during her forty-nine days before transitioning into her next life. The only time I felt her was when I was folding laundry in the bedroom, my back to the wall and facing the doorway. The dog we had just adopted for my soon-to-be-stepdaughter was sitting in the window's light. Suddenly, he stood up on his hind legs and "danced" the way that my grandmother had pretended to do with him in the few times she'd seen him before she died. Then she was gone. So, to remain as close to her as I could, I beckoned our dog Conan with me everywhere I went in the house, and he gratefully accepted my nightly snuggles as loving defense against the nightmares.

Within the grieving, my wedding planning persisted. My mother was excited when I asked her for help in finding the green and yellow áo dài that my bà ngoại had described. "Those were your great-grandmother's favorite colors," she explained. "The green was for the colors of the bottles lined up on a fence on her street in Việt Nam. Yellow for the flowers." Until that moment, all I had known about my great-grandmother had been the image of her in the black and white portrait; she grimaced and her knee-length gray hair was wrapped in a bun that she would later shave to mourn the death of her husband. Now my inherited memories of her had color.

CHAPTER 19

I went online to pull up pictures of Vietnamese brides so we could narrow down the styles. My mom's excitement faded into "hmmm" and "okaaaay" elongated in doubt until she spotted a picture of an obese woman squeezed into a custom sewn áo dài. The custom sizing chart recommended at least six Xs to fit my boobs alone. "That might fit you," she said. Anxiety building about my body and my unspooling connection to my heritage, I put off dress-shopping for months, until I could no longer stomach everyone asking, "Did you find your dress yet?" followed by an uncomfortable smile or "uh oh" when I responded that I had not even started looking.

So like an "elite" Asian, I Yelped áo dài shops, and I drove us down the Little Saigon streets where my mother used to drive me weekly.

A handful of seamstresses greeted my mom and me with a confused look, as most people do when they see this small beautiful woman and then me—tall and freckled and round in the mid-section. When people find out that she is my mother, they respond in shock, "That's your mom?! She's so beautiful. You must look more like your dad."

At each shop, the seamstresses echoed one another:

"Do you know your size? We don't have anything here that will fit you."

"Áo dài does not come in short sleeves."

"Green and yellow are not for weddings. Only red and gold."

My eyes began to burn and well, and my body felt as if it were grotesquely engorging as it did when I'd suffer bouts of paranoia when smoking weed as a teenager—my nose widening until it consumed my face, jowls swallowing my already weak chin, belly fat gurgling as it stretched my skin and jellied my joints. I slouched a little more to hide my breasts, and turned my watering eyes away from the seamstress, pretending to browse through the racks of colorful silk áo dàis.

I walked out of the last shop, pausing at the curb to wipe my eyes. "I know, it's so hard," my mother said from behind me. "People always say that I am too skinny, too small."

I swallowed the words that I wanted to spit about the years of hair-pulling, on top of the bouts of eating disorders, self-harm, anxiety, and depression that she had never seemed to notice, or at least never addressed. "I'm done. Forget it," I said. My mom told me to stop, to wait, and said the most motherly thing I've ever heard her say: "I named you Jade because you are precious."

I wanted to hug her and reminisce about all the times we'd gone up and down Bolsa, when it was just me and her, snacking on pastel bánh bò and shopping for knock-off Hello Kitty stationery and herbal medicines ground and wrapped up in paper packages that promised our healing. But I only responded with silence.

"Let's go to another place," she urged. "This lady is a bitch anyway. Did you see her eyebrows? Like drawn on by a blind dog." A smile tugged at the corners of my mouth. I turned the car around and followed my mom's vague directions and hand-waving.

Tucked into the corner of a mini-mall on Bolsa, Diem's shop was thick with incense smoke wafting from the altar and the loud crackle of Vietnamese radio where her husband hunched reading *Người Việt* newspaper. Diem emerged from racks of color like a glamorous drag queen taking the stage. In her skintight lace camisole, she bounced and pointed her manicured hands, waving away my mom's concessions that I was older and bigger than most brides. "The kids born here," Diem said, flipping through the racks for sample cuts, "marry older because of education." She pulled an opened-neck, three-quarter sleeve áo dài from the rack. "I got married older only because I was busy making trouble." Her husband behind us snorted without looking up from his newspaper. Diem held the áo dài up to my body, and it dropped just above my knee. "Us American kids," I tell her in Vietnamese, "drink too much milk too." Diem looked me in the eye and laughed. Her eyes traveled down to my breasts and said, "If I can get boobs like these, I'll drink more milk too." My mom cringed and I smiled. I liked Diem.

My mom pointed to the tiaras in the glass case and told me about how she wore one when she married my dad. I responded that I know because I had looked at those pictures hundreds of times, confused by all of it—the juxtaposition of two disparate parts of my life standing there next to each other, feigning happiness, my mother's pregnant belly barely showing through the flowing gown. "I wanted to look like a princess. A simple princess," she said. My mother assumed that people were always paying attention to her. I did not inherit that. My default is invisible.

CHAPTER 19

Diem ushered me back to the fitting room where she simply closed the curtain around me and I struggled to remember how to put on an áo dài. It had been years since I'd worn one, let alone undressed in such close proximity to my mom's critical eye. As I pulled up flowing yellow pants and slipped on the long green tunic with a stream of beaded yellow flowers down the front, I noticed that none of the hems, sleeves, collar, or zippers were finished. It was a rough cut, but I'd never been to a tailor before, so I had never felt uglier or fatter or more gullible. The fabric was shapeless around my body and I looked wide, more so because of the bright colors that my grandmother requested and that I, feeling foolish, took to heart.

On the other side of the curtain, the tailor told my mother in a low voice, as if I couldn't hear, "It's easy to make dresses for petite women like us. Skinny is easy. But your daughter is so big I have to be careful." Echoing between her words were memories of my mother's voice saying, "Eat all of your dinner and I will love you."

I pulled back the curtain and Diem went to work pinning. She and my mother talked about the pictures on the wall. The dresses were scandalously slitted up the leg and plunging at the neckline. "I was looking at these photos," my mom told Diem. "Is that you, Chị?" The seamstress smiled as if she was waiting for us to notice.

"Yes, when I was fifty," and she disappeared into the back. I watched my mom calculating years in her head. She called to Diem, "Chị ơi," still calling her older sister, "when did you come to the States?"

"The '90s," she shouted back. "To have my kids." Holding the hem of the satin yellow pants off the cheap carpet covered in lint and loose thread, I watched what looked like jealousy cross my mother's face. Diem was younger and more confident than her, had been able to spend more of her life in Việt Nam but still have her children in the States. Diem returned with a lacy red bustier with thickly padded cups. "I made this in Saigon. I'm wearing it to a party tonight," she told my mom. "With a skirt," and she used a red fingernail to trace a hemline right beneath her buttcheeks.

"Wow," my mom said in her polite voice that I knew meant shit-talking was coming later. "Sexy quá! You still look so young." My mom looked at me. I could see she was done with feigning girl talk, and the competition had begun.

"The áo dài I was going to wear to her wedding is too big for me," my mom boasted. "I'm twenty pounds lighter than I was when I had it made. I'm only ninety pounds now. How much do you charge to fix it for me?" They bantered back and forth, only noticing me when Diem poked my right breast. "This one more big," she said in English.

She slipped her hands inside the loose collar of the áo dài and the polished tips of her nails clicked as she fiddled with my bra. "You're not wearing it right," she said. She struggled with the hooks. "You're creating fat rolls that are going to ruin the shape I'm sewing into the back of the dress. That will make it look," she switched to English, "not good." I caught my mom's wince in the mirror. "Nhưng mà," Diem conceded. "Your shoulders are narrow. Very feminine."

"See?!" my mom exclaimed. "That's good!" The only body parts I had clearly inherited from my mother were my hands, but I'd calloused the fingertips and chipped the nails from all the hairpulling. Now the shoulders. But no one ever says you're as beautiful as your mother because of your shoulders.

At the very least, someone could have mentioned that the dress looked nice. Or that I made a good choice to honor my grandmother's wishes and my great-grandmother's green-and-yellow spirit. There was no "say yes to the dress" moment in which my mother dabbed away tears because I looked like a princess.

Instead, I was reliving all the hours my mom made me spend in mall dressing rooms with her during my childhood. Always looking at her, trying to give her reassurance she never had, but inevitably failing. In the same way, I spent my whole wedding dress experience obligated to compliment two old women battling each other with their memories.

By the time Diem was ready to hand over my final áo dài a couple of weeks later, I was exhausted from the whole process. I didn't tell my mom that the dress was ready. I just went by myself to pick it up and limited my interaction with Diem to a cold customary, "Cảm ơn, Cô Diem," and nodded to her husband still behind his newspaper.

CHAPTER 19

In the weeks before our wedding, Mike and I were both startled awake by running footsteps pounding down the hallway toward our bedroom. We whispered to each other that it must be our daughter who sometimes shuffled to our room sweaty-headed asking for water or to be tucked in again. A full lights-on check showed her sleeping soundly in her loft bed. I could see in Mike's eyes the fear I had been feeling from the nightmares. He had heard the footsteps on his own. It was getting stronger.

I was still plagued by *Paranormal Activity*'s storyline of a poltergeist that followed a woman. Had a spirit from my grandparents' house, or even further back from Việt Nam, followed me all these years? Would I not be able to create a home? Was I doomed to be haunted? Was it the curse of being the eldest daughter of an eldest daughter?

Mike and I heard that our house's original wife in the nursing home had passed. Both of them were in their-our house now.

Desperate for restful sleep and a sense of safety in my own home, I did the hardest thing: I asked my mom for help. "Fruit," she said. I would've laughed if I wasn't so scared. "C'mon, Mom, they're Catholic. Fruit?"

"A lot of fruit," she continued. "A whole plate of nice ones. Light some candles and then talk to them."

My eyes welled up. This was not going to work. "And say what?"

"Tell them the truth," my mother said in a way that I will always remember. "Tell them you love the home they built. You are getting married, and you will take care of the home. You will love your husband and raise your children in this home. You will make them proud that their home is now yours."

I'm sure my mother saw in my teary eyes a look that she had seen many times before—that I didn't believe I could do it. "Just try," she said.

So we did. Mike and I put out fruit and candles. With an arm around each other, we spoke to the husband and wife who built the home we were trying to live in.

When brides think and talk and post about the plans for every minute detail of their weddings, I just don't understand. In every other facet of my life, I am an overthinker. But there was no Pinterest vision board for our wedding. Aside from browsing áo dài designs, I searched once for "wedding hair styles" and gave up on the first page of results because I figured all of them would be impossible with my sparse hair. I only searched a second time because of that little bit of hope that convinced me a braid with some extensions woven in could hide the bald patches. Then I gave up. I'm a quitter. Some might think that my education and career confirm otherwise, but in many ways of the heart, I run away.

This is the attitude I embodied when I walked into my appointment for the hair and makeup test. This is not something I would have ever done if my aunt-by-marriage was not a professional makeup artist. For ten years I had avoided salons, along with dental appointments and facials and any other situation in which a chair would lower me and my head into full view. I did everything I could to prevent others from seeing my hair, from feeling uncomfortable or curious enough to ask what had happened. I could not lie about thinning my hair by my own self-hating hand. Every Tết, I cut my own hair. First with the bowl cut–straight bangs of my childhood, and then when my hair was too thin, just a simple scissor saw of my thin ponytail. My head was always lighter when I bowed to Phật Bà, thanking her for keeping me alive for one more year and sneaking in a prayer that she would help me finally stop pulling out my hair.

My aunt glued and re-glued different false eyelashes that looked like children's drawings of setting suns. They weighed my eyelids down and pinched the lids. "The rest of the makeup won't look right if you don't have lashes," my aunt reassured me as I struggled to keep my eyes open to this cow-lash vision.

"I look stoned," I said to my reflection, "or like I have an eye infection."

"You're just not used to it," my aunt said. I'd always been on the outside of beauty and fashion. Aside from the few punk rock years when I experimented with rainbows of eye shadow, I ran in the opposite direction of the women in my family, away from mirrors and makeup and, in general, drawing attention to myself. At the same time, I hoped that my aunt and her hairstylist friend's movie magic could help me look like not a beautiful but at least an unremarkable bride.

CHAPTER 19

By the time my aunt's friend came in to test out different hairstyles, I had surrendered to the false lashes by closing my eyes. She must have mistook this for relaxed because her fingers started dancing through my sparse field of hair before I had enough time to properly brace myself. So it hurt more than my walls of disassociation would typically allow when she said, "Your hair will never be the same."

"Will the braid in the pictures I brought work or not?" I felt the air ripple and thicken in the wake of my business voice. One of my trauma gifts is barreling over people in a workaholic avoidance of my vulnerability.

The hairstylist sucked her teeth as she shuffled through my photos. "I'll see what I can do."

She combed and twisted and piled my scarecrow hair but could not conjure enough volume to mimic anything near bridal. After rummaging through her rolling suitcase of tools and supplies, she emerged with a bottle that looked like a cross between nineteenth-century perfume and pesticide sprayer. "This is a hair fiber spray," she explained. "It will give your bald patches some color and texture that look like hair." She spritzed into my palm a scattering of staple-sized dark brown fibers. I rolled them between my fingers. They were coarse and pokey, and I envisioned the ascetic hair shirts I'd read about in a medieval literature course. Was the hairpulling and all these moments that resulted from my self-inflicted balding my version of penance? For what? What had I done? Why did every "normal" experience—wedding, haircuts, showering, going outside on a windy day, sitting still for five minutes without ripping hair from the roots—feel like torture in my body?

Like a graffiti artist, she sprayed onto my bald patches the artificial hair fibers at varied distances and pressures. When her brow unfurrowed, she handed me a mirror. Up close, my head appeared painted like the morose-looking accountants in the Just for Men commercials from the '90s. The fibers added some texture, but no more than a hedgehog's coat. I held the mirror as far away from my body as I could. I swiveled my head back and forth to see my un-hair in different lights and at multiple angles. At that distance, the mirror did not catch my difference. "Whoa," I said. I nodded at her. "Thank you."

Right before our wedding ceremony at our home, I peeled off the false lashes and their gummy glue because they overpronounced the scarcity of lashes I'd had for nearly two decades. I filled in the space with more of my own eyeliner, and I added a yellow flower to my sprayed-on hair, as was one of my great-aunt Adell's posthumous wishes, channeled through the medium.

My dad got emotional seeing me in my wedding áo dài. It was surprising because I'd never seen my dad cry, let alone hear him say "I love you" (one thing my parents had in common). But here we were, me standing in my wedding dress and my dad choking on small talk.

My mother entered the room. She pretended she didn't know who my dad was—the same person she'd been writing letters to, even recently, about how terrible I was, the same person she had been bad-mouthing ad nauseam for my entire life. There was no way she had forgotten his teeth ("so big"), his forehead ("even bigger"), or his chin ("where is it?") that she had been seeing in mine for as long as I'd been alive and wishing that I wasn't. In this moment, she tried to weaponize her illusion of forgetting to dig at my dad-me. Because how else do you celebrate your daughter's wedding day? "Oh, hi," she said, clasping her hands and bowing slightly like a nice Asian. "What your name?" My husband-to-be laughed in disbelief, and I shook my head of fake hair as my dad played along by introducing himself and reaching out to shake the hand he'd once put a ring on because I was growing inside of her.

And, yet, she did take me into another room and had me crouch down so she could reach my neck where she strung my bà ngoại's jade Phật Bà pendant. Like my grandma, this pendant was glitzy and glamorous in gold and diamonds. It was heavy and strong around my neck. This one would not break. I began to cry. "Stop it," she said, starting to cry as well. She added.

I asked both my mom and dad, who apparently had just met, to walk me to our backyard where Mike was waiting to exchange our vows. But before we could, Conan trotted up and lay down between us, as if the ceremony was for him. My stepdaughter, in her own gilded floral áo dài, pointed and giggled at our silly dog. Through everyone's laughter, I felt the safety and protection I had been craving. Mike and I held hands. He loved me in my

CHAPTER 19

áo dài, my one wedding dress. Here was our dog. This was our family. This was our home.

In the photos of the reception, there were so many people from my maternal line that you could hardly make out our faces in the wide-angle frame. All of my Vietnamese relatives, save for my youngest uncle and aunt, rearranged tables so that they sat away from everyone else who was playing cornhole and giant Jenga. During the brief rounds I made in between anxiety attacks and subsequent emotional eating locked in our bedroom, my mother made sure to convey the scattered Vietnamese mutters questioning why I only wore áo dài and not a Western white dress as well, why I had the event at home, why I wasn't doing formal greetings bowing to the elders. She took away.

In our speech to our guests, Mike and I thanked everyone who came from near and far (cousins traveling across continents to be with us), our parents for raising us into people who loved one another, and, finally, to those who couldn't be present but who were always with us, especially my bà ngoại who had chosen my wedding dress for me. As I said this, I glimpsed my mother touch her face. She added.

Mid-reception, she clasped my arm above my elbow and whispered that I should change. "Just looking at you makes me sweaty," she said, just as she did when I was a kid and my hair fell across my face or matted to my neck. She took away.

So I changed. Into a black dress. But I kept the yellow flower in my hair.

Once we were married, the footsteps, the heaviness, the nightmares—it all stopped. The fruit and the truth worked. Even for a Catholic. She added by taking away.

PHOTO ALBUM 3

Well after the customary forty-nine days of grieving my grandmother's death, I helped my aunts and uncles clean out her house. The wall and ceiling above her altar were stained with incense smoke from her prayers to pictures of people she knew and some that she didn't. The latter were the ones she was not letting rest. She prayed to them asking for winning hands at the casino, for vengeance, for longer life. With her gone, they hovered. They were the heaviness in the air, the weight and tingle on my neck and shoulders.

While I was in her house rifling through trash and bags of pills, they cracked a wooden cabinet in half, knocked the pictures of Buddha and Jesus off their nails, and sent the dogs whimpering right back over the threshold. I hurried and mumbled prayers to keep them away as I dug through the closet.

I found boxes of pictures and remembered my grandmother clicking in new flashbulbs into her camera. She wanted a picture of everyone. Some photos were bound face-to-face in twine or wrapped in singed foil. But every picture of my mother was untouched, unlike what she'd thought. She'd assumed Bà Ngoại had been casting curses on her for years, blamed everything on it. But here were pictures from my mother's life before me—no

PHOTO ALBUM 3

black magic, just memories and secrets:

<table>
<tr>
<td>

My bà ngoại supine,
Child-mom's naked
splash in waves
On Nha Trang's smooth shore.

She does or doesn't notice
White men watching, their
eyes blurred.

</td>
<td>

Sad woman and boy
Who could be my uncle's twin.
Mom shushes me, "No!"

Grandpa's bastard, no secret.
Glad but guilty he chose us.

</td>
</tr>
<tr>
<td>

Viet Air Force pilot
Staring into horizon
Cap tilts, medals wink.

He beat mom's "elephant" face.
Nose jobs remember self-hate.

</td>
<td>

Tall, lanky muscle
Bowl cut and basketball shorts
Another dead uncle?

"Your mom thought he was
your dad,"
Uncle says. I keep this one.

</td>
</tr>
<tr>
<td>

Old West studio
Sepia toned, she poses,
Ruffled Southern belle.

Like Bonanza or Little House,
Surviving in a new world.

</td>
<td>

The first in color,
My mom peeks from
behind bangs
Hibiscus in hair.

Hawai'i made her look happy,
And she's never taken me.

</td>
</tr>
</table>

I am holding these black and white memories, but they are not mine. I bought an album for them but struggled to arrange which faces side by side.

Anyway, I didn't know who I'd show them to. So I keep them in a box too, far away from the altar, far from where I'd ask for any answers.

As for all the videos and CDs, I donated them to the Vietnamese Oral History Project archive at the University of California, Irvine. I hope they are making someone else dance, remember.

CHAPTER 20

LETTER TO A MỸ LAI MOTHER

You've always been asked-told you are "Mỹ lai," meaning American, meaning white. You've always been halved.

Even though we share the same body, you won't remember me. Because we became unrecognizable to each other. For what felt like an endless period of time, despite the fact that, by the calendar, it was only a year—the first year that your firstborn won't remember, at least not well enough to articulate.

Brace yourself for the body-racking cry in the parking lot where you click the test results that confirm your unborn child's sex is female. You cry from the fear you are not strong enough to protect yet another in a line of firstborn daughters from a culture that erases you by calling secondborn sons "Anh hai," from a world that relentlessly terrorizes girls and women. You cry from the shame of being afraid to be and birth a girl.

CHAPTER 20

The pregnancy, though, is the happiest extended time of life. Even through all-day sickness for months and incessant fears of worst-case scenarios in between the reassurance of ultrasounds, you indulge in all fruits and enjoy your walks to synced heartbeats. You have purpose: to live.

When it comes time for a baby shower, you ask your mother twice if she'd like to be involved in the planning. You are rejected twice. You offer her an alternative: shop with you to create a registry. "Why would I do that? So awkward." She will continue with a familiar refrain: you are American, and she is Vietnamese so she just doesn't do these kinds of American things. You ask your Vietnamese American friends if their mothers believe in baby showers and are regaled with stories of extravagant gender reveals and buffets and tiny áo dàis. Your auntie and close friend generously step in to organize and host the shower where your mother will whisper complaints to everyone that you did not include her in the planning. After the party, you find the baby book that your mother made for you, and two pages are dedicated to photos and detailed notes on who gifted what tiny things at your mother's own baby shower.

During the thirty hours of labor, you hear multiple women enter the room next to you, scream for a few minutes, and then get carted, with their newborn babies, to a recovery room. The delivery nurse tells you, stuck, that you don't seem like the screaming type.

Your dad and in-laws spend the night with your stepdaughter in the hospital lobby. Your mom only shows up twenty-eight hours into labor when she hears you will need a c-section. You'll see her face in passing as you are wheeled into surgery. You ask the doctor to not let her in.

The first words you say to your baby when your husband brings her fresh red cheek to yours: "Con ơi, Mẹ nè." You'll whisper the same to her when nightmares wake her, when the dog's barks at the mailman startle her, and whenever she needs you in times in her life that you cannot yet see. Don't get in your head about why your Southern Vietnamese mother passed down "Mẹ" to you, and so to her, instead of your regional "Má." Just say it. Enjoy the pleasant surprise of how instinctual—imperative—it feels to speak to her in the same language that ushered you into the world.

The first smell of her is liquid and new. You read that animal babies smell their mothers for food and protection. Your bà ngoại is eucalyptus oil, Marlboro smoke, and CVS perfume; your mother is Oil of Olay lotion, artichoke tea, and incense. Stop yourself right here because you're starting to beat up your body for not being like one of those girls who smell like coconut shampoo or plumeria body spray all day. You are not the chicken stock and pencil shavings you smell in your sweat. Your body is putting your mind through a lot. Smear some coconut lotion under your nose and do this: send home the baby's first worn onesie to familiarize your rescue dog with her scent. He is the one who crawled into your lap on his first day in your home, peed on your hand out of excitement, of claiming you. You are making shapes of memory: a triangulation of smells—her to him, him to you, and you to her. Remember that you are making, not destroying. Remembering is what is going to help you through this.

The first time you want to face someone while sleeping is with her. Feel her slow breath on your face. You'll want to roll the shape of her nostrils around in your mouth, hold them between your teeth, feel the loving tension in your jaw. Let that fill the emptiness growing inside you, the hole that's getting chipped away by all the words from parenting advice books and other

CHAPTER 20

parents who try to convince you that sleeping next to her is bad—"individual," "baby," "independent," "healthy."

This is the cold tongue of America. Your ancestors slept side by side from birth and that did not make them incapable snowflakes. They were survivors with the memories of their mothers' breath in their nose, the shape of her in their bodies. She's going to want that, too. She will sleep best with your hot breath on her skin. You've been tilting your head away but she stirs and reaches until you are face to face and you can't hold your breath any longer. You'll breathe into each other's faces. This will be hard because you can't be invisible anymore. You can't give into the pounding "I want to die" thoughts.

The first is always going to feel like the last. It's okay to take too many pictures of everything she does. When she looks back at the scrapbooks you've curated (even if you're making them as if you're already dead), she'll see it as love, not fear.

You're afraid of losing her. You'll regularly feel like she's slipping away, but you're the one. So, stay.

Remember how you used to spend hours drawing pictures of families, all with the same hair and eyes and last name? You topped these stacks of drawings with a title page with the name of their town: Strawberry Fields. Your white TV dream. Even within the family you choose to create, people will focus only on your daughter's blue eyes or her light skin and tell you she is

"So pretty. She must look *just* like her father." They'll look back and forth between you and say, "She's *so* white." All the nannies at the park assume that you are her nanny too. When you dress her in áo dài for Tết and she loves it so much she wants to wear it to the park, on walks, to the beach, brace yourself for people who will only see a white girl playing dress-up, who say, "Cute costume!"

Because you've been halved, you never expected your children would look like you. After all, you don't look like either of your parents, not without study. You thought that your genetics would be swept away, like the "bụi đời," the "dust of life." But it still hurts that people don't connect her to you, like she's been halved again, diluted. And here you are using this language in your head when you look at her through others' eyes.

Remember that her father is your partner. He is the only person who can most fully see you, reminds you that of course she looks like you, but that you have always been made to feel invisible so even you cannot see yourself in her. Cling to him and the few others who see that her facial structure—the shape, her chin, lips, nose, and forehead—are yours too.

You must learn to parent in a partnership, which you have never witnessed in your own family before. Being part of a team with your husband will be the most unexpected daily challenge. You will catch yourself parroting your mother's resentful critiques of her children's fathers that cast herself as the victim, all of which is deeply rooted in her never feeling cared for by her own mother, let alone the father she never knew—the sabotage stemming from great pain. She was trying to break cycles by giving you a father but ended up

CHAPTER 20

ripping him apart every chance she could. Because of how burdensome this made you feel as her child who needed her, you will never ask your husband for help when you need it, but also relentlessly ask him if he is mad at you. Even when he assures you that he isn't, you will catastrophize by assuming he is leaving, so you prepare to leave first. During arguments, you are eerily calm. This will be important to know about yourself.

One of the scariest parts of being in love with the person that you created a child with will be that you are so afraid to lose him or let him in that you refuse to show happiness. Just as you choked on words while around your mother, you will feel paralyzed from greeting him when he comes home from work, and you won't be able to articulate what life-preserving joy you feel when your baby smiles or kicks or touches your face. You reject his compliments because you feel like you don't deserve them, because if your own mother can't love you, then how could anyone else? It is too scary to be seen, not only as yourself but now also as a wife, a mother, a center instead of a side.

You think all the nice things he says to you are a lie because all you can hear are your own deafening thoughts: "They'd be better off without you. I want to die. I want to die. I want to die." Because you think he is a liar, you will grow angry with him, and then feel more alone. You will hate when he asks you how your shower is. What are you supposed to say? That you showered in the dark to dull at least one of your senses because the water on your skin is so painful as it grates your bleeding nipples on breasts that will throb and buzz long after nursing is over and salts your aching, itching c-section scar? That the laughter of teenaged boys huddled outside the closet-turned-"lactation room" at work makes your breasts pound in pain even more? That your wrists and your teeth ache? That the water makes you too painfully aware of your exposed biology?

Your body is changing, but not in the ways that people tell you it will. There is no peeing when you laugh, no crying at rom-coms. In fact, you don't laugh or cry at all anymore. And there is no lingering baby weight. In fact, you lose fifty pounds and everybody compliments, "You look great, Mama!" What they don't realize is that everything sweet tastes sour, everything fresh tastes like its rotten future thingness. You don't eat because that's your way of edging toward disappearing.

But your baby eats well. She craves fruit, vegetables, and more fruit, even the grinding seeds of kiwi and dragonfruit. It seems that the sadder you get, the healthier and stronger she grows, making it feel like this is how it is supposed to be.

The dog who side-eyed you suspiciously when the baby kicked him through your stomach now barks a lot, at everything. At first it seems sweet that he is protecting the baby, and you read an article about how they have evolved to mimic human faces. You realize that he is mimicking you—curl-lipped snarl to hide a trembling whimper inside.

When the baby smiles or laughs with other people cooing to her in English, try not to take it personally or as a threat. Her doing so will not negate that you are her one and only mother, the one whose palm on her back or fingertips tracing her barely-there brow immediately consoles her.

CHAPTER 20

It's not worth it to snap at all these people who seem to be encroaching on your baby. They assume that because you are now a mother you are a good person, so when you tell them to shut up or bat their hand away from her, they are extra disillusioned with this whole motherhood thing.

You're gonna feel like you're shattering everyone's world, but remember that it takes a lot longer to build a lie.

When your mother says she doesn't receive text messages that you sent about a medical emergency that prevents you from visiting her, you send her an email (because talking is too painful) asking if she can come visit you and the baby, maybe once a month. You include your work schedule so she knows when you'll be home. Be prepared to double over with nausea when you read her response: "I'm not sure I like it when my own children preaching me about how, what, where, and when I should do certain thing for someone. I have enough of that kind of shit from my own nutcase mother-She had me gone through hell and come back to this life. I will do how, what, where and when I am good and ready. That could be tomorrow or that could be never." In the wake of her words, you'll lose hair and sleep and moments with your baby that you won't get back.

When your husband pleads for you to get help, don't take it as a criticism, or as some extended form of colonialism trying to "fix" you. He is hurting too. Remember when he said, "I miss my wife." The therapist will start by giving you tests—the Edinburgh Postnatal Depression Scale and a few other fill-in-the-bubble metrics. You rank off the charts, a point under recommended hospitalization. You also score an eight out of ten on the Adverse Childhood Experiences (ACE) questionnaire. "Such a model minority," you joke, but she doesn't laugh. "You know, high test scores," because something about you lately just wants to keep digging in deeper. "Aced 'em! Get it?" The only thing that saves you from hospitalization is the fact that you are still taking good care of your baby.

The therapist scans stacks of self-help book chapters on PPD and worksheets to track your mood. Most of them are obvious—eat, sleep, exercise—that you won't do because you're already bored with the simplicity of this therapy. She suggests bougie solutions too—maids, day care, hypnosis for trauma. You're not going to pay anyone to help you. You're already feeling equal parts proud and guilty that you've made it far enough from the projects where you grew up to a neighborhood where people walk dogs in sweaters, where you have a yard that she toddles around and you follow her with sunscreen.

You will desperately build puzzles to feel in control of the spiraling pain. Completing and framing cats in libraries, cats in kitchens, cats everywhere will even make you feel like maybe pulling hair is okay. Sure, you like it. When your dad gifts you a puzzle of '80s nostalgia, you wonder if this means he can see how desperate you are to live another day.

You will start to take medicine. Everything in your head is going to call this a validation of your weakness, of giving into the colonizing doctors that your mother warned you against. But, in a way, she's actually the one who pushed you to get that prescription. It was in a presentation for your students that you share statistics about how Asian American women have some of the highest rates of depression and suicide, and that's just the ones

CHAPTER 20

who report it. You realize that PPD is part of all those invisible numbers, that your mom is one of those, that you are becoming one like her.

You worry that, because she hurt you as a cry for recognition that she was hurting, you will continue this cycle with your own daughter.

The last time you were medicated you were a teenager, back when Paxil was new. One pill numbed you into a vegetative state, another into a manic flail, and the last that made you hallucinate. The new one evens you out—"I'm glad I got my wife back," he tells you. The only side effect is that it makes you remember dreams from years ago, and your mind is compelled to recall them from beginning to end: Zombies blare music from their gaping chest cavities until you baseball bat them into floating ash; your beloved LaKeith Stanfield is gunned down in a drive-by shooting and you escape the flying bullets in a Willy Wonka-esque candy glass elevator; you climb a concrete mountain to a Hindu temple where you drown in a puddle of rainwater and incense smoke. You know, dreams.

With the help of medication, you've had to remake yourself, figure out what motherhood is for yourself. You retrain your tongue. First, stop mumbling "I want to die. I want to die. I want to die. And I'm going to kill myself."

Second, relearn your first language. Read to your infant daughter all of the bilingual Vietnamese books that you discovered from Gemma's Library and Tiny Wrist Co. You will get frustrated. There will be tonal waves of phrases you've never used before. Do not forget the shame you feel for all the times you've corrected your mother's pronunciation or laughed when she said, "I need ketchup. Let's go to Chik-a-Flik." You know now that it felt like love but sounded like hate.

There will be other words that you'll realize are simply complete blanks for you, like "rainbow" (cầu vồng) and "giraffe" (hươu cao cổ). Learn what other words you know look like in print on the Duolingo app, and be patient with the ridiculous sentences spoken in Northern accents: "The fish bites the bicycle," "She speaks Vietnamese because she is Vietnamese." Once you get past the initial laughter, resist spiraling into the existential crises about how Duolingo's words for "you" and "me" were different from the "mình" you grew up saying for "me-us." You will, but try not to, take it personally when the app's sentences seem to mock you: "I am forever in the kindergarten," "I am still normal," "I am not normal." "Who am I?" "Your question does not have an answer." Instead, pluck from these phrases what you want to impart to your daughter in your ancestral language: "normal," "answer," "forever." Study these words and repeat them to her proudly so she can name the world, and herself, in ways that you couldn't. When you get lines in her books down, read them to her in happy tones of voice that you've only heard in English. Help her love Vietnamese by showing her it loves her.

After your family scatters following your grandmother's death, cope with the loneliness that the only person you can speak your mother tongue to is a baby who is just now learning to respond with hums, points, and knowing looks. You'll yearn for the sound to an embarrassing degree. Once when you took your baby to the nature center where you heard a family complaining to each other about how hot it is (aren't you from

CHAPTER 20

Viet-hot-and-humid-as-hell-Nam?), you pull your resistant baby—flower-eating, dirt-digging earth child that she is—away from the pinecone display and start talking look-at-me loudly to her about con chim (birds). "Oh wow, con chim bay lên trời!" and you look over your shoulder like a doofus clown to see if they heard you, as if they'd pat you on the back or invite you over for a dinner of cá kho tộ (because damn you miss the taste of your mom's cooking) or maybe adopt you and give you a Vietnamese name that sounds like waves when you're floating on your back, like Lien after your cousin who is such a good person and mother with gentle voice and you only wish you could be so inherently good. But they don't. Of course they don't. You should know by now that Vietnamese don't praise, especially not in public.

Your mom always told you that Vietnamese culture does not praise children because it will make them turn out the opposite. "Say beauty and come out so ugly." So you accepted it when your mother told you your nose was big and fat like her original one, and she pinched and clothespinned yours in an effort to make it thinner and higher. When your daughter arrives with a near exact replica of your nose, your mom says, "She like Jade. No trouble breathing," looking at your husband for a laugh. He doesn't and never will. You thought you would struggle with resisting the return of the nose pinch, but the first time she reaches for the baby's nose, you quickly and easily bat her hand away and tell her to never do that again. Never refer to your daughter as "lớn/big." Tell her, in both languages, that she is strong and healthy and beautiful.

You don't tell her that being a mother is realizing you've been mothering yourself all along.

Your mother embarks on a tour of Europe a week after you give birth.

What will help you combat the feeling of impending, continued loss? Because all of the women who came before you are a part of you, you feel their losses from war and immigration and abuse. You feel your own repeated losses of doubled identities and the memories that slip away because you're always shifting.

But listen more carefully. This new life is more than just echoes. Hear her when she calls you Mẹ. Hear her when she calls you Mama.

Write to yourself as a mother and a daughter. Write so that you don't forget. Write so that, even if silence grows between you (and this is your greatest fear), she still cannot forget. It's okay that you write in English and only occasionally in Vietnamese. Trust that your bilingualism will double your chances of articulating your love for her and accurately curating, in fact and in feeling, the happy memories that you build together each day. These journals and scrapbooks that you fill will be her history whenever she doubts who she is, who you are, or fears the outlines of things that already make her whimper in her sleep before you rest your hand on her chest and allow yourself to breathe against her cheek.

CHAPTER 20

On your first Mother's Day (prepare for this to become the loneliest holiday of the year because, even when you are a mother, you're still a daughter too), flip through the stacks of scrapbooks—these distinct shapes and sounds of your memories as mother and child—that will be the unspoken echo of your first words to her. "Con ơi, Mẹ ne." Not halved, but doubling.

CHAPTER 21

THERAPIST 6 AND THE ANTEATER

"Then beneath the colour there was the shape. She could see it all so clearly, so commandingly, when she looked: it was when she took her brush in hand that the whole thing changed. It was in that moment's flight between the picture and her canvas that the demons set on her who often brought her to the verge of tears and made this passage from conception to work as dreadful as any down a dark passage for a child" (Woolf 19).

Elderly white women fascinate me. On the one hand, there is a nostalgic pull based on my paternal grandmother and my great-aunt who grandmothered me after her sister's death when I was only six. Though they weren't lovey-dovey women, they had cuddly cats, wore soft sweaters and colorful jewelry, made holidays and birthdays with personalized gifts and desserts, let me eat any and all sweets on a daily basis, and smelled like . . . warmth. On the other hand, the old white ladies who patronized the "General Store," literally what it was called to harken back to the prairie days of the customers' youth, where I worked in college were downright nasty. One entered the store in a cloud of floral perfume and a tinkling of gold jewelry. Peering over her bifocals, she looked up my

CHAPTER 21

apron—old timey atmosphere—to my face that she didn't look at again as she launched into her tirade. "My Precious Moments angel figurine was cracked when I opened the box at home. It's porcelain! How do you explain yourself? It wasn't broken when I bought it. You boxed it—"

"No, sorry that wasn't m—"

"You *should* be sorry!"

"I wasn't apo—"

"You owe me an apology and a full refund. My grandchildren will be so disappointed when the new angel is not in my curio cabinet when they visit. And it's all your fault."

I refused to say sorry to this woman. "Let me get my manager," I smiled. She came out and apologized profusely as she processed the refund and filled out the order form for a new stupid figurine. It was in these old white women that I saw everything my mother warned me about in American culture—having everything, collecting the world, and still complaining.

Of course, as the first American-born child in my family, I was implicated in this national reprehensibility too. So it was with an anchor of self-loathing that I introduced myself to the old white woman who was in charge of treating my postpartum depression.

Her office was decorated with pewter elephants, wooden masks, obsidian statues of elongated bodies, and mosaics of colorful glass in Turkish lanterns. She seemed to have paraphernalia from every corner of the globe. Taking a seat in her office made me feel like another collectible, an exhibit in the world made a zoo. At the same time, my internalized colonialism surveyed every decoration in awe. *This Karen is cultured*, I thought.

Her clothes were flowy and light. She seemed to glide instead of step. She appeared ethereal. Her white lady magic lulled me into sitting on her Tibetan meditation cushion long enough for her to interrupt my admiration of her elephant figures to ask, "Hypnosis?"

What little I knew of hypnosis came from spectating the side stage at the county fair during my one-week summer with my dad. The hypnotist convinced audience participants to act like Madonna or bark like a dog when he snapped his fingers. Everybody thought it was funny, but I was mystified and horrified by this black magic. When my dad pulled my hand skyward when the hypnotist asked for volunteers, I slumped into the dead weight protest that kids do and when he finally let go, I swiveled and urged him toward the strawberry shortcake stand.

Obviously using her black magic to read my mind, the hypnotherapist said, "I know that hypnotism gets a bad rap like it's just some carnival sideshow." Her eyes smiled and one of her bracelets tinkled as it tapped against the teacup she began stirring. "But really, hypnosis is just listening to my voice." I started feeling warm and loose. "It is my voice that will guide you toward the rivers of thought that are always running through you." I involuntarily swayed as if my bà ngoại in late-night prayer. "We'll focus on bringing you to the riverbank. Your toes will touch the water. There you can hear the current." I was Madonna. "It is then that you can break the dam, set free those thoughts that keep you hairpulling." That word was my snap. I broke out of the womb this woman created with her open-air market trinkets and tea-soaked voice. I was back in my body and the shell went back up. I was back to being a patient. My body curled in on itself.

"You've just had a baby," she said, smiling at me in a way I'd never seen my own mother do. "This is a time for nurturing and regrowth. So let your body do what it is made to do." She was trying to comfort me. Though I craved comfort from everyone in my life, whenever it was offered, I rejected it. I could not help but interpret her words as criticism. I could not even let my body do what nature had created it to do. I could not care for myself as I should, and even though I was taking care of my baby, I was not enjoying it as I should. I had failed to outgrow this hairpulling that had started with puberty. I was a fail—

"You like the elephants, don't you?" Jarred, I nodded. "What do you like about them?"

My mouth hung open as I struggled to downshift my bullet train of self-berating to controlled, measured conversation. "I like," I cleared my throat, "that they remember." She waited, as white women tend to do to get you to do what they expect. I continued, "I read about an elephant that walked miles to the funeral of his trainer. She didn't just remember where to go, but she remembered the person."

Karen nodded and stirred her tea. "Hmmm."

CHAPTER 21

"One time, at the zoo, I saw a young elephant get its foot lodged in a tire that had been strung from a tree for them to play with. There was a huge cloud of dirt when all the other elephants ran across the enclosure. They surrounded the little elephant and used their trunks to pull its foot out of the tire. He was free in under a minute."

She looked into me. I wondered if she wanted to demand a refund of her time with me.

Instead, she said, "I think you might like an anteater too."

"An anteater?"

"When you feel those intrusive thoughts, the ones that don't stop, the ones that make you want to pull your hair out to distract from the internal pain," she sipped her tea, "think of the anteater. Think of the way it sucks up ants with its snout. Your intrusive thoughts are the ants. You are the anteater. *You* can control your thoughts."

I envisioned the anteater. All I could picture was its snout vacuuming one of my white hairs with a quick plop and suck. Then, I imagined its snout sucking out all of my white hairs at once, the bouquet of roots waving. I concentrated on anchoring my hand on my lap, away from my hair.

"Great," I said. "I love it. I think that will really help."

I didn't return to Karen's office, but I researched anteaters, or ant bears as they're sometimes called. They can slurp up so many ants because they have oversized salivary glands that coat their tongues to stick to the insects' bodies. They are extra.

I learned, too, that anteaters are good at swimming, but they don't often swim. When do you see anteaters near the water? No, they're most often found nestling in loose dirt and shallow leaf beds. After digging for ants all day, they are satisfied to rest on the surface.

But to witness a dissatisfied anteater is unsettling. At the Santa Ana Zoo (a crowded plot of land along a freeway), I watched an anteater pace the perimeter of its enclosure, bobbing its head, and then retracing its cyclical steps. I looked for a zookeeper. No one was around. Kids didn't want to watch a stir-crazy anteater. I stood there watching it suffer, already resigned to the fact that neither of us could do anything. What happens when an anteater runs out of ants?

INTERLUDE-
INTRUSION

Bubble Boil Boil Boil Course Course Surge surge surge
To fingertips
                                      Cut

Lady aliens in *Alien Nation*
Ripley in *Aliens 3*
Robin Tunney in *Empire Records*
Demi Moore in *G.I. Jane*

Natalie Portman in *V for Vendetta*

Nemari in *Raya*

"Nothing had shaped itself at all. It was all in scraps and fragments"
(Woolf 90).

CHAPTER 22

THE WIG

No one looks at me anymore. At least not in the way they used to. Not that that was the way I wanted to be seen. But there are no more catcalls, no more heat from strangers' eyes traveling up and down my body. The depression exacerbates the undesirability because I don't shower on account of the debilitating nausea at seeing my own naked body weighed down by despair, so what little unwashed hair I have left is greasy and stringy. My chin acne flares up because I don't drink water because I feel like I don't deserve it and my breath tastes (and I'm sure smells) sour. My weight fluctuates wildly, and being on the heavier end of the scale almost feels comforting in that it keeps people further away, yet I still long to look like a movie star or my mom in all the pictures of herself.

On account of aging out of visibility to men (and, so, women too), I started pulling my hair more, not necessarily in public, but in less privacy—in the car during traffic, in my office at work, on the couch with the hand farthest from my husband. I couldn't wait for moments alone, which, in a life with young children, were fewer and farther between. The urge was overflowing out of secret spaces.

Shaving my head was tempting. I craved freedom from the constant urge edging into every daily motion from adjusting my glasses to sitting on

CHAPTER 22

the toilet. But, at this age, I feared a bald head would elicit undue heroism. People might assume I was a cancer survivor, and their eyes would trail from my scalp to my non-mastectomied chest. October would be confusing. I felt preemptively guilty for being presumed brave and strong. A freeing shave was not an option.

Instead, I fantasize about a body that is before all the hair I've pulled, all the sleepless nights that have dimmed my eyes, and all of the wanting to die that has curved my spine and anchored the corners of my mouth. I remember at twenty parting my hair down the middle into pigtail braids for a day of volunteering at a summer writing program for inner city elementary-aged children where my ability to teach second-graders poetic devices, my summer shorts, and no doubt my long handles of hair caught the eye of one of the hunky program coordinators. In other times, I was hit on by a guy at a rave who bore swoon-worthy likeness to a young Ice Cube, was subject to countless whistles and increasingly creative offensive comments like "Can I get some milk?," and dated a model-handsome plumber who couldn't spell more than a three-letter word in Scrabble but boasted that he dropped all of his other girlfriends to date me. This was the body that demanded the attention of men who my mom taught me were the goal.

I also fantasize about a body *after* hairpulling. Maybe if I find the right metaphor in therapy or the right Korean hair growth serum at CVS, I will have hair again. Maybe I should venture into one of the gentrified neighborhood's "beauty bars" for eyelash extensions. Maybe I wouldn't be so embarrassed when people looked at my face if I just risked leaning into the stereotype of middle-aged Vietnamese women by getting my eyebrows tattooed or microbladed. (My mother did eventually come to terms with my first tattooing, years later saying, "Well, I guess tattooing my eyebrows is not so different." She never said a word about any of my other tattoos that followed.)

Maybe if I deprive myself of enough food, water, and sleep, I'll waste down to a size that no one will notice the hair so much anymore.

The wondering, the conditions, the obsession with what hair is there and not there—it's a simultaneous living and dying. But nothing is certain. I don't know if tomorrow will break my hairpulling habit or me.

As a teacher, part of my job is to pretend that I know something, anything. This was a familiar farce to me in living a life of always trying to prove that I was worthwhile. I read this book: love me now? I got this award: love me? I worked twelve hours a day every day for ten years: love? After those 43,800 hours in the field, I risked admitting what I had learned, which was that I knew nothing. My confession took the form of an assignment with the deceptively boring and technical title of "process analysis." In my introductory composition courses that every student begrudgingly must take, I try to dismantle all the bad feelings about English teachers as red pen–wielding grammar hounds and of college as an elitist gatekeeper. Undoing all of that educational trauma is impossible, but I try to make my students feel more welcomed and empowered with an assignment in which they write a second-person narrative about a process they are proud of having completed. They essentially advise their younger selves through the process under the idea "If I knew then what I know now."

The resulting essays floored me. The severity of their struggles outmatched only by the depth of their resilience humbled me into not pulling—that is, at least until I scrambled to write words to express the ineffable. And then grade.

During the COVID pandemic's shift to online education, I was relieved that I could adjust my camera so that my balding was not as evident. I could remain fairly unseen. Until the one process analysis essay that changed everything.

CHAPTER 22

"You are Luke Skywalker beginning your journey in a barren desert. Except, you do not get to pick up a lightsaber. Instead, your hand forces hair to come out of your scalp. You cannot tell which hurts more, the scorching rays of the sun, or the stinging of the hair that has lost its home, and the feeling of a rope-burn on your fingers."

> Thank you for making us the hero.

"When your mother yells at you to get your hand out of your hair, try not to get mad at her. It is entirely possible that she is in more pain than you, although she has a funny way of showing it."

> You are so forgiving—and loving—to your mother.

> Me too.

"The name of your disease is harder to pronounce than it is to understand, and the side effects of your depression medication are not mixing well [. . .], leading you into a rage overdose."

"Learn how to comb your hair. Sweep it to the left, sweep it to the right, consider getting a mullet. Your hairline is receding faster than a forty-five-year-old man's."

> You do so well with capturing the simultaneous closeness to and distance from your body.

> I admire your bravery in writing about this.

"You write down these small victories in your online journal, one that nobody else could stumble upon, attempting to stay positive besides repeatedly getting the short end of the stick. But, don't allow these victories and tricks to inhibit you from making friends. You find it hard to let people in, not because you don't want them, but because you fear that they won't want you."

THE WIG

It was overwhelmingly heavy to read the trichotillomania struggle as it happened to a student I cared about. Her words ignited the full-body itch of needing to pluck. It doubled: my pain, her pain. Why didn't I ever commit to shaving my head completely? Could doing so assuage the relentless compulsion? Then, I imagined all the stares, all the questions: "Cancer?" I'd disappoint on multiple levels.

> "Although you fear the judgment of strangers, remind yourself that any judgment they could have will be no greater than how you have judged yourself."

Skylar was brave enough to, without hesitation, spring for a wig. I was at once shocked and inspired that she was able to admit her-our hairpulling problem to a stranger at a wig salon. If she could do it, should I wear a wig too? Should I at least invest in a weave or extensions? I should try, even if just to earn my role as "teacher."

Wow . . .

Oh.

> "You became confident. [. . .] But, most unfortunately, you became a liar. Self-preservation became your crutch, and you felt guilty for finally feeling beautiful. You wear a wig, and it weighs you down like an anchor."

> "Your wig will work no better than a Band-Aid on a gunshot wound if you don't deal with how you feel internally."

Oh no . . .

But I was the student. I learned the heart-dropping gamble of the wig as a thousand-dollar investment. My anger snowballed. For Skylar, for me, for all women seduced into the capitalist beauty system that charged them to add hair to their heads and remove it from everywhere else on their bodies. All this time and money spent on changing ourselves, especially those of us

CHAPTER 22

deficient in lashes, brows, and hair. Then we'd just throw away every tube of mascara and lip gloss and roll-on this and powder that. Plastic colonialism.

What would I model for my daughters about how and why we cover up and change ourselves?

In her powerful storytelling of her experience with trichotillomania, Skylar taught me that I needed to "realize that you are more than what your illness says you are." Like her, I needed—desperately—to "wield your story like a saber."

One of my first teachers, my dad taught me to ride a bike by taking me to the top of a hill at the end of my grandparents' street and telling me to let myself fall. "When you get to the bottom," he'd said, "just keep going." I learned how to ride a bike. It was late, but I still could go places.

CHAPTER 23

CRADLE CAP

After a pregnancy of Del Taco runs and insatiable impulses to laugh at my own fart jokes and fight strangers, we welcomed our third daughter into the world in 2019. Her personality from womb to world remained the same. The nurse who bathed her shaped her thick black hair into a mohawk that stayed, in spite of any subsequent washing or brushing. It fit. So we let it.

Although our histories mark March 2020 as the beginning of the COVID-19 pandemic, our baby and I knew that it had already begun. Visitors were prohibited during our stay, and only my husband was allowed to visit during the afternoon. He would return home at night to care for our other two daughters.

Our youngest daughter and I were alone a lot for the first couple of days of her life. She was born rock and roll, but there was a peace between us. I nursed and snuggled her, I read *Bless Me, Ultima*. We watched the Food Network. I did not pull my hair. Mostly, I stared at her miraculous face. The racialized words that I was familiar with but would never say to her at risk of replicating my own "tragic bụi đời" liminality tumbled around in my head. *She looks so "Asian." So much more Asian than me. Those eyes. Her nose. That hair. So much black hair.*

CHAPTER 23

I'd had a scheduled c-section based on the struggles with my last delivery that also led to surgery, but the baby and I were physically healthy. Plus, I was hypervigilant in an unrecognizably mentally ill kind of way, so when the doctor came in a few hours after the birth and I was not only up and walking around but also cleaning the room, she said, "You're not the kind of woman I can convince to rest, are you?"

Mohawk and I were discharged two days early.

I was happy to leave the eerily visitorless hospital and the inescapable cloud of sanitizer. I was riding the wave of peace from our first two days together and feeling more prepared for what was sure to be the next round of postpartum depression. And I was. We were.

By the time she was growing into her third month of life, her eyes were bright to the point that multiple people remarked on their shine, their liveliness. Her smile was a full-faced experience. But her scalp was beginning to dry and flake and then grow the yellow crust of a cracked lake bed. Under the advisement of our pediatrician, I rubbed a variety of natural oils on her scalp, and she enjoyed these massages, closing her bright eyes and smiling. The dry lake bed remained. In fact, the crust grew thicker. It absorbed the external oils and her own. It began to smell. When I Vietnamese sniffed-kissed her head, there was no more natural baby smell. Her scalp smelled like the puss that oozes from blister and infection. She smelled sick. And it made me itch and squirm with anxiety.

Our pediatrician had a file of surveys that ranked my postpartum depression off the charts. For the second time.

But she did not know about my trichotillomania. Or, at least, we hadn't spoken about it. I assumed everyone *knew* just by looking at me. So, our doctor couldn't have known what a mental and physical shock it was to me to ask that I remove our daughter's cradle cap crust by hand, as well as the hair that would go with it.

The first time I did it, I used a special cradle cap comb. The soft bristles were powerless against her thick shell. This was not going to be textbook. I was going to have to use my hands. I waited until she slept and her chubby cheeks twitched with dreams. With the same hands I'd learned to distrust for their uncontrollable abuse of my own body, I edged a fingernail under the lip of her cradle cap and shoveled a millimeter at a time, all the while watching her microexpressions and ready to shift to smooth scalp strokes if her eyes fluttered or mouth started rooting. As much as I had no hesitation to hurt myself, I was so afraid to hurt her. She kept dreaming. I kept digging. The yellow crust on her scalp lifted like at a fault line.

My entire body seized when a tuft of her soft baby hair lifted with it. Nausea surged through my body to see my own hands uproot hair from our baby. I was committed to only touching her with love and protection and comfort, yet now here I was having to peel and pluck her fresh, vulnerable little body. What's worse, deep inside, bubbling up in that coursing arterial rush of the imperative to rip my hair out was a satisfying relief to watch my daughter's scalp and hair fall into a pile of sluff underneath her still-sleeping head. I liked it. I liked scraping away this dark hair I'd guiltily admired for looking "so Asian" and this layer of scalp that was the first part of her body we saw emerge from my own. It was a hairpulling that was care.

After weeks of peeling away the plates of the cradle cap's regrowth, her head was pink and shiny and healed. Her hair grew in full and layered with colors.

"For how could one express in words these emotions of the body? Express the emptiness there? . . . It was one's body feeling, not one's mind" (Woolf 178).

PHOTO ALBUM 4

Mom always told you it was bad luck to have pictures of three so here is the fourth full of your fear of forgetting in too many pictures in which you're not there because you're taking the pictures so that when you are dead what you want them to remember about you is how much you saw them and all these fun photographed moments will be the truth that they don't question the way that you always doubted your own memories and even now you wonder whether they will remember you as a good mother because if you really were good wouldn't you just put the camera down but at least their childhoods are documented because like your great-aunt modeled for you in her scrapbooks of all the wars and her safaris and her cats like her you saved every photograph that is so expensive because no one prints pictures anymore and every scrap and remnant of napkin ticket stub pamphlet sticker for every birthday holiday trip and every first second third fruit eaten leaf collected dog kissed and every other moment when it shifts to past tense because Vietnamese taught you it's all about tenses so out of fear that you might die any day now and leave for them the seed of doubt that their mother didn't love them enough to stay and because Woolf reminds you that "Love had a thousand shapes" you chronologically order all the stacks and stacks of drawings that show scribbles to human forms to faces with emotion and bodies in movement and all of us together talking in dialogue bubbles in one "Love is forever" and in the responding bubble "Keep trying."

CHAPTER 24

THE SUM OF DIRT

If I was not always thinking about pulling my hair or if my bald spots are showing or what I should eat to make my hair grow back faster, I think I would be much better at math. Once, in elementary school, I was the only girl who made it "Around the World" in the multiplication game of the same name. I would have started a second circumnavigation of my classroom had it not been for Armando whose friend whispered to him the answer to "8 x 7" before I could overcome the overwhelming self-doubt that always accompanies my successes. It was around then that I stopped being good at math. I struggled through high school and college to pass the same level of algebra. Math was not something for good, but for meticulously counting and recounting my steps, or making sure the TV volume was always on an even number.

But now, numbers mean more. This is the math I know:

CHAPTER 24

0 people in my family look like me +
1 hundred and 70 centimeters to tower over my mother +
2 hundred pounds I tip and no one recognizes me as hers, as Viet +
3 degrees that teach me the words of Black Queens who wrote about not belonging +
4 people needed to make a photograph, my mother warns-promises, "less unlucky" =
10s of thousands acts of hate I feel vicariously—a word always attached to living is now trauma.

Countless are the number of people who've asked me what's wrong with my face. Subtract that same number to get the zero people I've told that my face is the sum of all these bad things that have happened in and around me—the tally of war, soldiers and bar girls, mass death reflected in the glints of green in my eyes as they blink open. I've never said what's *really* wrong because, in the too many seconds it takes to muster courage, they've already forgotten me.

In the microbiome, I'm not the only invisible life. In the microbiome, we're all a minority. The skin we live in is not fixed, but moving, crawling, floating in the wind, thirty-seven million per hour. The parasitic mites eight-legging it through our eyelashes are gone from my ripping because I've never felt like part of this "we" that science now uses to pretend it hasn't been a tool of racism throughout history.

In that story, I'm dirtier than the rest. I'm "bụi đời" outside and in. I'm inherited yellow peril.

You can't see the virus—endemic to a homeland I can only visit—teeming inside of me, just the dirt on the Victorian sexy part of the neck when I can't bring myself to shower, until that uncle strokes it and asks why I flinch. The pumice stone I use to scrape the dirt off my body disgusts too. The vesicles, remnants of nature accelerating too quickly, trigger trypophobia—a fear you must see, not of what it is, but the pattern. The repetition. The numbers.

You'll hear it in the auctioneer-fast disclaimers in every pharmaceutical commercial about my-our disease that makes every other part of life risky, that forecloses chances of frolicking in fields. You'll hear it when I tread data and disclaimers in between flirting with a new sex partner, and the echo in the splashes of their vigorous scrubbing afterward. You'll hear it in the doctors' (judging) voice about my 17 million viral load ("Are you an IV drug user? Are you a sex worker? . . . Oh, you're just Vietnamese"). You'll hear it in their instructions in milligrams, blood tests, and ultrasounds sonaring for death and not a baby because (the savior cautions) avoid sex, drinking, bleeding, licking. You'll hear it in all of the extra testing and Health Department phone calls when babies grow inside me—my ancestral revolutionary thrust, resistance in rooting gums and puckered thighs fat with survival.

As maths work in balance ("both sides of the equation," I hear my former teachers echo), what you hear will be muted by a silence that grows between me and my mother. With estrangement looming, my health problems multiply: spikes in my liver's viral load that had been "unidentifiable" for a decade; kidney stones that extend my chronic stomachaches through to my spine, inducing nausea with my favorite fruits and vegetables and making even water unpalatable—my body's rejection of the natural; sudden A1C surges into prediabetes that force me away from the foods that were the lingering tether to Vietnamese culture, making me feel like a traitor on another level; polyps, polyps, and more polyps; gums that recede and bleed around teeth that I've clenched and ground down into flat, chipped, enamel deficient smile inhibitors; a recurrence of chondromalacia—a degenerative cartilage condition—in my popping, slipping knees that I hadn't experienced since I was a teenager being told that my mother didn't like me; an undiagnosable simultaneity of heaviness and instability in my legs that leads to a fall slamming my head into the side of a car and then concrete for my first weeklong dazed and disoriented concussion; and, the most unsettling, an irregular heartbeat that jumps into my throat choking off my breath into the stillness of a French art film only to be broken by humming-bird speed palpitations. My paternal grandfather had five heart attacks in the latter half of his life, and my ông ngoại . . . well, that column on my medical chart has always been blank. What did I inherit from this stranger, the one whose anonymity and absence kept my mother's heart broken? Did he get sick or die in a way that would foretell my own death?

CHAPTER 24

The doctors, whom I distrust but make appointments with for the sake of my children, farm me out to specialists who draw blood, run scans, grope and squeeze, and furrow their brows. "No cancer," they report, as if I am to be grateful that this is the reason they dismiss the persistence of all my symptoms. Nothing, they tell me. Without numbers, without proof, it feels as though my body is killing itself to say that I am a bad daughter who deserves to die, and a mother whose children are better off without me. During the COVID-19 pandemic, I feel like I'm beginning to die of something deeper, and I am a number not being counted. The numbers.

We are the fastest growing population within these borders paid for by wars with our blood, treading waters lapping from lost homelands—Philippines, China, Japan, Korea, Vietnam, Cambodia, Laos—and I am one of the over two million Vietnamese in the US, the majority (only here am I a majority) in California. We are the percentages that defy the limits of 100, but so do the surges of hate against us within the borders: 361 percent, 527 percent increases in "incidents," and what does it mean when a number on a scale undoes itself. Odd.

The meaning of 10,905 fists, tongues, triggers, eyes puncture us with hate, and that's just the number reported—scratch that, the number just went up like the flames on the shuffling old man's shirt—as history weighs our countless heads into a bow, pinches our lips into the silence that you think we hold by blood, but if you'd ever heard the din, the clamor, the discord, the motherfuckin' ruckus of Auntie's kitchen, Uncles' squatting card game, Sister's screams in her pillow, and the Mother: the fracas, the fray, the fear, the fight. Even.

The numbers. Xấu số. Sixty-two of our women named victims: more than 40 stab wounds in Christine Yuna Le, 35; more than 125 hits to the head of a woman, 67; more than 10 shot at the Chinatown subway stop, trains still shook from Michelle Go, 40; more times than you could count, the names of the pizzeria owners who saved her are printed and pronounced more than Eun Hee Chang, 61, stabbed by 3. Odds and evens, the days keep passing, and I only call or text my mother to remind her to be safe and offer, to her refusal, to use my white-passing privilege to get her groceries in safety.

They—we—are murdered and the world keeps moving on through

its forgetting, so it wouldn't matter if I died, right? The lack of coverage makes me feel like even my own children wouldn't miss me if I died, so why not? How many more die before we tackle why so many of the attackers are Black? That our shared enemy is white supremacy pitting us against each other?

The enslaved. The lynched. The underground. The _____. The egg fermenting over the centuries it takes to speak the score. In the wait, pop the yolks. Let them bleed and feed. Eat. And I will love you.

During the pandemic and the riots responding to George Floyd's murder, my husband and I focused on surviving. Our bags were packed and escape strategies planned. Mike started baking bread from scratch. He filled our home with the comforting smell of rising dough and butter. He fed us during hard times. Just as Great-Aunt Adell had foretold. Fulfilled promises kept me going.

On the dawn of the Year of Quy Meo, 2023 (odd), I read the news of the Monterey Park mass shooting. Eleven elders died on the beginning of Lunar New Year that belongs to all of us—the Water Cat (or Rabbit, because we're different too) that comes every twelve years.

It wasn't the gun violence that was so shocking. Over one hundred mass shootings just in the first two months of 2023. I already had plans for where to hide my children in the few places that we frequent post-quarantine—this closet and that recess, behind the school's air conditioning unit, in the reeds at the park. The planning led to more plucking.

What shook me was that it was New Year. Tết. The one time of year that even my mother was all smiles, that promised me a new beginning—that is to say, an end to all that made me rip my hair out. Of the handful of traditions I'd been taught and had practiced for Tết was the tenet that the first day of the new year foretold the rest of the year. This year of the cat started with mass death. Of elders. Dancing. So close to home.

The next day, they found the shooter dead in a van by his own hand. He was Vietnamese.

My stomach sank heavier. They would write this off. He was an Asian who killed Asians, so it couldn't be an act of hate. He was from war-torn Việt Nam, so it was just his individual mental health problems. It was just.

CHAPTER 24

The pall was distracting. Bầu cua cá cọp stayed in its box. I opted for sweats instead of áo dài. The poppers I swept aside for a few days until I could muster hearing their tiny explosions. I don't think my girls noticed. I plied them with extra boxes of bánh đậu xanh in their lunches, and an extra two-dollar bill in their red and gold li xi envelopes.

Luckily, a local botanical garden seemed to suddenly realize they were in the middle of a county full of Asian Americans and held its first Lunar New Year celebration.

The entrance was flanked by dozens of security guards. To enter a *garden*, one that we had visited just weeks ago, we now had to empty our pockets and bags for inspection. Though my husband doesn't know many Vietnamese words, he is fluent in my hand gripping his arm right above his elbow. Mike clasped my hand in reassurance before we had to star our limbs for the metal detector wands, our children watching. "Why do you have to do that?" our youngest asked. My husband and I assured her it was to keep us safe, but it didn't feel that way. We all knew why the added security was there, but I didn't hear anyone say anything about it. There was no mention of murder as our daughters visited booths to meet a hefty rabbit snuggled in a stroller decorated as an altar, watched a calligrapher brushstroke velveteen ears and wishes for good luck, and played games of picking up tiny objects with chopsticks. The girls were laughing and loving it, seeming comfortable in celebrating the lunar new year while also enjoying the exploration of a completely Chinese-centric celebration. I hovered. When other parents got too close, I yelled, "Watch out!" When their kids cut in line, I elbowed back in front of them, saying loud enough for their parents to hear, "Don't stand by and let people cut you." Our girls were quiet. When the high school students volunteering to run the booths did not give our daughters the same attention as the other visibly Chinese kids, I went behind the tables, got the art supplies or chopsticks myself, and loudly said, "When no one helps you, you do it yourself."

I felt other mothers staring. Even though there were several mixed faces there, I felt like the biggest, most grotesque, and loudest bitch in the crowd. But I did not, could not, relent. I was in hyper protective mode because, for every young face I saw, I glimpsed it smattered by a spray of bullets, flesh chunking away in the wind to reveal bone. The bones are the same. "What color is bad luck on New Year's?" a high school girl asked our five-year-old daughter with the promise of a Chinese coin. "White," our girl said with her hand out, the empty square framing the soft flesh of her palm.

The dragon and lion dances were our pandemic-era children's first. They rose from their seats, mouths agape, as the dancers twisted under an open sky. The speaker behind me pulsed bass at a decibel that felt like it was tenderizing my organs, and I worried that I wouldn't be able to hear or feel danger coming. But I pretended. When some of the lion dancers launched into a breakdancing interlude with some kids from the audience, I acted like I was having only fun. I showed our daughters how to cross their arms b-girl style and sync their bodies to the beat. They smiled and moved to everything but the beat, and this made me smile. My surge of happiness ran electric, parallel to the fear that the b-boy's legs twirling and unfurling from his head-spin would spray blood into the young faces in the crowd. That the wind would carry it. That we would all be marked.

But it didn't. None of that happened. My husband drove us home, my heart seizing at every passing car and through every intersection, while our children sang and ate cookies and asked questions back to a podcast about axolotls that, they learned, can regrow any part of their body.

All that remains are the crinkles in our children's yellow and red arts and crafts from my clenched fists.

CHAPTER 25

DEAR ZACHARY LEVI

Dear Zachary,
I just finished your book *Radical Love*. I'm wholly thrumming from it. First and foremost, thank you for the bravery, emotional labor, and spirit of caring (for yourself and readers) that you invested in sharing your experiences with abuse, trauma, depression, and suicidal thoughts. I hope that you feel good, strong, for having written this book.

Your book resonated with me so deeply. The constellations of emotions you described were so complicated, yet your words rang with a clarity of heart that is really helping important epiphanies to crystallize for me, as I'm on my own journey with therapy for Complex PTSD, DBT, EMDR, and the rest of that jungle gym of acronyms.

It feels stiff, doesn't it? The opening of this letter? That's not me. Or at least,

CHAPTER 25

not the part that I wanted to show you. It's just what I've been taught to sound "professional." Or mentally "stable." "Worthy" of being listened to. I'm just trying to do different. Because I've done this before, written letters to a celebrity. I was a kid before. I thought that celebrities were special, so if I could be seen by someone special, then I would be too. What is it that I want now? The desire to be seen and special feels the same, but it's also different. Now, writing to you is writing to myself is writing to my children is writing to my childhood self. It's all there—here—in what you wrote.

The echoes in our mothers' manifestations of intergenerational trauma are uncanny: from the mercurial moods, the compulsive shopping and subsequent hoarding of things that she couldn't let go, the distrust of Western food and medicine, and masterful manipulation, to the wishes we were dead, threats to career and relationships, and even the public humiliation about bed-wetting—all encased in the shell of more kindness and compassion for anyone other than her own children.

All that you described in your book—the self-castigation, analysis paralysis, feeling like a failure, struggle to accept care, funny façade to alleviate and mask loneliness, and the desperate thoughts of not wanting to live but also not wanting to die—I've felt too. I am feeling it now. I'm feeling that everyone would be better off without me, that it would be like that scene in Disney's version of *Alice in Wonderland* in which the lizard chimney sweep Bill gets sneezed out of the White Rabbit's house by a giant Alice, and everyone watches him careen into a speck in the sky only for the dodo bird to dismiss his loss with a short, "Well, there goes Bill." And back to the narrative.

This feels dangerous to think, feel, write. If I admit that I trauma bond with you, a white man, does that solidify that I am a traitor? Stepping out on my culture? Am I choosing the easier, well-worn path? Will this way erase myself as a way to disappear? Again? Do I want your power of hypervisibility? Your power to write a beautiful book filled with sentences that made me laugh and cry in times that I could not otherwise muster either emotion? Why am I hit so deep when and how you use verbs like "cratered" and enunciate your "fuck"s in your audiobook (what better than to hear your voice tell me it's going to be okay)? Are you just another white writer—Herman Melville, Sherwood Anderson, Virginia Woolf, Anne M. Martin, Dean Koontz, Kevin Smith, and so many others—whom I've wanted to become, maybe in part because I would never be fully represented, let alone accepted, by them?

I am writing to you, a white man, and before you a white woman who made me want to be a white man (or an Asian woman), and before that a white boy. So maybe this is not about transcending race at all. Maybe this is more violence I have learned to do to myself. Even my fantasies are the torture of invisibility and unrequited everything. Maybe the fact that you're a rich white man is what makes you able to draw out of me all the ways I've been silenced; you by being you makes me feel powerless, so bonding with you somehow equalizes our power. Maybe, Zachary Levi, what I have to learn from you lies in everything that has not been given to me.

Before, when I wrote to Rider Strong and Angelina Jolie and other *Tiger Beat* stars who didn't respond to my purple bubble letters, I couldn't see them the way I see you in your social media. Mostly your shitposts of mental health aphorisms, '90s memes, dad jokes, and videos of elephants startling each other with their trumpeting farts make me smile, but every once in a while I sometimes see you posting in real time while I'm logged in, and I get a tingle in my chest knowing that we're on at the same time, looking for something. It's in the rare and fleeting stories of yourself that I can see our shared pain lingers. In your panoramic videos of open landscapes—a snow-blanketed mountain, a Mediterranean shoreline, a vast Texan field—you are alone. Sometimes I catch your shadow as you pan

CHAPTER 25

across the landscape, the wind beating. One you captioned "Home sweet home." Does the quiet bring you peace? Does it give you respite from people whose expressions and words make everything we've been through simmer and splash?

I'm obsessed with seeing the same things that you do because in some weird transversal you see me too. Do you notice when I click the heart within seconds of your posting it? Can you feel the radiating of my heart in the way that I hope my kids sense me kiss their cheeks while they're sleeping?

Do you realize that when I see you post, it's a reassurance that, even though you've wanted to die, you are still going, and that means I can keep going too, that I can keep living in the same world you do? I hope you can feel, in some cosmic telepathy that is all electricity much bigger than our skin can contain, how deeply I yearn for you, for me, to keep living.

> *"Both of them looked at the dunes far away, and instead of merriment felt come over them some sadness—because the thing was completed partly, and partly because distant views seem to outlast by a million years . . . the gazer and to be communing already with a sky which beholds an earth entirely at rest" (Woolf 20).*

I heard you asked on a podcast when was the last time that you didn't feel enough and you replied that it was that morning because you don't yet have a wife and children. I can teach you something too: a family does and doesn't save you. The children will exceed the notions of love that you write about—they'll explode it in solar magnitude, daily—and, in doing so, they will trigger everything we didn't have. Everything they do and don't do can activate the feeling that you're failing as a parent, just as you felt like you failed as a child. And, as with every failure, you'll jump to your own suicide as a solution. Parenting is a perpetual cycle of falling in love and grieving. It is so emotionally overwhelming that I find myself wanting to observe my children like a movie, how I want to be like Huck Finn by observing everyone's reactions at my own funeral. This is the closest I get to understanding or empathizing with my mother—how loving a child resurrects the deepest pain. But I refuse to let my pain kill the love I bear for my children. I can't. Won't.

I can see the negative impacts my condition bears. When I pull my hair, my sassy side-footed Dachshund mix begins to shiver and, on occasion, gags. I drove my dog to vomit. Co-regulation is not working for us. Instead, I'm ruining him. Like I seem to do to everyone else and every other situation. Does your dog sync with your nervous system too? Does your Australian Shepherd help alleviate your loneliness? My fantasies revolve around simply having a full head of hair, lush like your dog's fur, and talking with you without having to explain any of the things I'm tired of people telling me that I need to talk about. No more, "What's wrong?" Or, "Are you okay?" And then the inevitable string of "It's not as bad as you think./Things will get better./You have so much to be grateful for./You are—" I want so badly to escape this routine (and the noise it creates in my head) that sometimes I listen to your voice singing on "I See the Light" and squeeze back tears: "Now she's here suddenly I know / If she's here it's crystal clear / I'm where I'm meant to go." I want to be with you not in any romantic way, but to be understood without having to talk anymore. My fantasies are to be alone-unalone in the quiet open landscapes.

All of this therapy is about the body now, regulating our nervous systems wrecked by our mercurial mothers. I listen most closely to a podcast episode in which you speed-talk through Buddhist tenets of freedom from desire. Sometimes, when people realize that I'm Vietnamese (okay, when I tell them), they tell me they love Thích Nhất Hạnh. I am never sure what to say, only resolute that I can't confess how my knotted insides unspool and I want to drop to my knees every time I hear his quote, "our wounded child is not only us."

CHAPTER 25

In your book, you explain how, even when painful to do so, you set boundaries with your family: Mother. Child. In some ways, it must be easier for you to preach love and forgiveness because your parents are dead. I haven't spoken to my mother in over a year (that's two zodiac animals' worth of misfortune), not since things fell apart among the found objects painted onto the canvases of Ann Phong, whose exhibit I thought would bring me closer to my mom. It was there that I had to reckon with the fact that I've been living in a self that is, as the monk foretold, her shadow. I drew a boundary by saying "no" when she started talking about suicide in front of my children. She pouted and huffed and refused food for the rest of the afternoon that I hoped would be a treat for all of us. A week later, strings of long text messages called me disrespectful and a drug addict and a high school dropout, accused me of lying about her, and, in co-opting the slogan of the Stop Asian Hate movement, lectured to me that "Hate is a Virus." The pain was debilitating, and I know that the vitriol of your own mother's letters helps you understand that, even though I wrote a long response to her, I never sent it. Instead, I kept silent. I could not engage further because being criticized by her on top of the harshest criticism I inflicted upon myself would surely kill me. It was already enough torture that I replayed the day at the Ann Phong exhibit—the last time I've seen my mother—over and over in my head every day since. She is often the first and last thing I think about every day. And every day I have been tempted to reach out to her, to swallow my pride and apologize, grovel, and accept all the names she called me as part of my identity. I hinted to my current therapist, who bears a nauseating resemblance to Olivia Munn, that I want her to make a choice for me. I could not trust myself to make the "right" decisions because all I could hear was the voice in my head that hated me and criticized everything that I did as wrong. Olivia did not choose for me. She asked me to listen to my body, to read it for myself. And it said "no." I still haven't reached out to my mother. Because what would I advise my daughters to do if someone, anyone, even (or especially) me, had treated them that way, not just once, but for years? I would tell them "no."

So, to parent myself, I said "no." I chose to be a "bad" daughter, the type that does the white American thing (the Zachary Levi thing) of marking a boundary and sticking to it. You named your mother's treatment of you as "abuse," not a child's duty or the culture. Trauma and culture have been conflated for me and caused a lot of internalized racism, self-loathing, and ultimately loneliness, but your descriptions of your mom were like the phoropter that sharpened focus on how to unbraid trauma and tradition. If our moms can traumatize us with such uncanny similarity but be from such wildly disparate backgrounds, culture is clearly not the (sole) root of trauma. With your words in my mind, I realized I could untangle trauma from tradition. I could be Vietnamese without her.

I cried after I finished reading your book and wrote you the first draft of this letter. (This is a rewrite. Of a rewrite. Obviously.) I cried for you and all the trauma you suffered. I wanted to hold you. Not just the you on your book cover where they made you look like a youth pastor—a "cool" one, but still—but all the versions of you. I wanted to hold your sixth-grade self being bullied after your newlywed mom moved you away from your hometown. I wanted to hold you after your mother humiliated you for wetting the bed. I wanted to hold you as a young adult receiving that long letter from your mom and stepdad, the one that I'm sure made your stomach drop with every hateful, threatening word. I wanted to hold you every time your mother showed more attention and care to anyone but you. I wanted to hold you when your mom bad-mouthed your dad. I wanted to hold you when you felt the distance cleaving you from your siblings. In making myself someone who could see you, I was holding myself. "Reparenting," Olivia called it. I was finding a way to mother myself so that I could mother my daughters in ways that none of the generations before had been able to. The ghosts were waiting to see, as a result of all their pain and sacrifice, how I would live.

> *"Through the crepuscular walls of their intimacy, for they were drawing together, involuntarily, coming side by side, quite close, she could feel his*

CHAPTER 25

mind like a raised hand shadowing her mind; and he was beginning, now that her thoughts took a turn he disliked—towards this 'pessmism' as he called it—to fidget, though he said nothing, raising his hand to his forehead, twisting a lock of hair, letting it fall again" (Woolf 123).

Is your book about wanting to die your version of my letters to strangers? If so, I replied.

I sent you a much shorter, much saner version of this letter, and I've counted the days, weeks, and months that you haven't responded—all the time that I've continued to add to this letter. And, yes, as I write and rewrite this, I realize that this is not really about you, a Hollywood actor who probably receives thousands of comments and DMs (and naked pictures) on the regular. The writing—the waiting—is how much I need to feel seen, if not loved, by my estranged mother. By myself. By my children.

"It was odd, she thought, how if one was alone, one leant to inanimate things; trees, streams, flowers; felt they expressed one; felt they became one; felt they knew one, in a sense were one; felt an irrational tenderness thus" (Woolf 63).

I'm trying to convince myself that your lack of response makes what we have ideal. I can bond without having to do the scary work of allowing you to get to know me. This is why I loved watching movies with my dad growing up. We spent our two days a month sitting next to each other in the dark, lights flashing across our faces, while my dad ate most of the popcorn and I ate most of the Raisinets. Then, like one of our favorite movies, the Quentin Tarantino–penned *True Romance*, we would get dessert afterward; we sat across from each other at a booth in Denny's or Ruby's and talked in the shortest of sentences about what we liked and didn't like about the movie. I thought I was connecting to the Hollywood stars and their characters without having to commit for more than a few hours, but it was actually my dad that I was distance-bonding with. It's like what your character in *The*

Marvelous Mrs. Maisel says, "Just do what I do. Stay away from people. If you're not around them, there's no mistakes to be made."

I've always needed to find meaning in the little things. Every little thing must mean something bigger about how I am connected to others and the world, like when my ears itch it means someone is talking about me; it can't be just earwax or a wayward bug that I dreamt through.

I dreamt of you recently. Usually my dreams involve drowning in my own feces and blood or failing to save infant versions of my siblings and children from natural disasters. But the other night, you intervened in the apocalyptic landscape typical to my subconscious. We sought refuge in a bookstore and, while tilting my face up to your height, I noticed that giant paper ships were suspended above us. "What if the Atlantic is the Pacific?" I asked you. Though quizzical, you smiled at me and touched my face.

This is the closest I've gotten to the prayer that you champion in your book. I used to have faith too. But it fell away when I had children and became more suicidal than I ever had before. Because how could that happen? And how could I keep performing a ritual that my mother had taught me, yet also abandoned me for European vacations both times that I gave birth? I've yet to return to praying at my altar that grows dustier.

The closest I've gotten to prayer is writing this to you because it's what is keeping me from dying at the hands of my own thoughts. This is why we pray, right? To stay alive? And to ask for the protection of others? Because I want to keep you from dying too. As my trauma-bonded twin, you worry me. I worry that I'll wake up to yet another notification on my phone about the suicide of a celebrity. Because Hollywood has shown me impossibility and possibility. So, even though I can never be like you, if you die, then I'm closer to death too. I want to pray-write to you in hopes that it will help you feel seen and cared for.

CHAPTER 25

When I pray, I ask a lot of questions. I guess they promise that we will keep going. How many times did I use a question mark in this letter?

Thirty. Even. Maybe it means something. If anything, I will keep counting.

It's happened. You recently posted a video of a New York street lined with brownstones and blossoming trees. Your caption? (Thirty-one.) "Me love you long time, New York." And, later, for some goddamn reason, you endorse a presidential candidate whose hateful rhetoric got so many people killed and left the rest of us living in fear. Dying happens all the time. You've died to me too. You were a part of me that I needed to write to and now you've reminded me that you are not me. You are your own person. There are some things I can't fantasize my way around, so my mother's horse—always looking back but galloping ahead—will run away from you too. I'm leaving you behind and taking *me* with me. After seeing your posts and subsequently unfollowing you forever, the sigh from deep inside me released something else.

It was my husband who recommended your book to me. And it was not for the stupid shit you said on social media. He recommended your book to me because, in your acute pain, he saw me. He's the only who has and stayed, held. All this reading and writing bound me closer to my one true partner. For this, I am not indebted to you because my people have been expected to kneel for too long, but it's something that happens when you find ways to survive: to transform pain into something beautiful.

Even forgiveness. For long time.

In gratitude for your book, this is the parting gift I'll give you—no, myself:

Our youngest daughter is twirling and singing through what seems to be the inevitable Disney Princess phase (despite our efforts to run this joint like Themyscira), and I admit that *Encanto* has been a healing arepa for my intergenerational trauma. Our girl's favorite character is Rapunzel from *Tangled*. She is obsessed with playing Rapunzel by draping blankets on her head, as well as becoming a "salon girl" to do my hair to make *me* Rapunzel too.

Trust that the irony that she most adores the princess with the longest, strongest, most magical hair is not lost on me. (Nor that Rapunzel was imprisoned by a narcissist who insisted on being called "mother.") Every time she hears your voice bust out that signature Flynn Rider charm and wit, the sweetest smile dances at the corner of her Nutella-smeared mouth. *Tangled* is, too, a major reason that she loves playing salon with me, so this hair movie you're in helped me get closer to her, and to myself. The other day we were listening to you singing on the soundtrack. She smiled. Then she held my face to hers and whispered, "Eugene is funny. He's a good guy."

The intimacy of playing salon girl stiffened me in the fear and shame of her exposing the bald scalp combed under my permanent ponytail. I refused, though, to show these feelings and risk tarnishing our salon. Though middle school drama class had proven that I could never be the performer I dreamed of becoming, being my daughter's confident salon client was my greatest acting role.

"What hair do you want?" she asked with one hand on her hip and a hairbrush in the other. I wasn't sure where a three-year-old got the directness and sass of the most veteran waitress in a roadside '60s diner, but I admired this about her.

I wanted to say, "any hair," but I asked, "What hairstyles can I choose from?" "Rapunzel or Rapunzel," she replied.

CHAPTER 25

"Okay, that sounds gr—" but before I could finish, she was batting my head with the hairbrush and dragging it through tangles so hard that my head tilted back. Despite how much pain I'd inflicted and endured over years of hairpulling, my threshold was crossed with the uninhibited hand of our toddler. Most wince-worthy, though, was when she parted my hair and I felt the cool tingle of my exposed bald crown.

"Mom, you don't have any hair on top."

In that moment, I fought back tears. Not for myself or my own pain or vanity. I wanted to cry because this brand-new person wanted to be a salon girl and wanted to practice her future with her mom's hair. I was letting her down. "I can't do Rapunzel hair," she said. It is without exaggeration that I mustered all of my mental and emotional energy to resist my impulsive responses to shut down or lash out. I clenched my jaw through the fear and shame, then released to open my mouth to a new inheritance.

"That's okay," I said and swallowed with the effort to invent a new experience in that moment. "I know my hair is different than you expected and that can be disappointing. But everyone's body is unique. Everyone's body tells a story about who they are. So does Mom's." Her lips still pouted and her belly bulged with that disappointed toddler posture. I concentrated and kept going. "You can help me tell that story if we work with the hair I have. See? The long hair on the sides and in the back?" She nodded and touched my hair, sending tingles through my shoulders and shins. "You are a very creative and kind salon girl. I believe you can do something cool with my hair. Salon girls like you are great because you help people feel beautiful. Are you ready to do that with Mom?" She nodded and smiled. She returned to her salon girl position behind me. Her little fingers rubbed my scalp smooth like the skin under a freshly peeled scab. I froze in letting her see and touch this part of me. She kissed my exposed scalp and then whispered in my ear,

"It's okay, sweetheart." She spritzed cool water on my head with a spray bottle and brushed gently until what remained of my hair was as smooth and straight as it used to be back when it garnered me compliments. She pinned flowers and bows in it from crown to split ends.

When she was done, she stood in front of me and looked me over. She beamed with pride. Her face was pure, uninhibited joy. Her eyes did not linger on the bald spots. She saw all of me. "You're beautiful, Mom."

"It was done," Woolf wrote for us, "it was finished."

INTERLUDE—INTRUSION

Pull

Push

EPILOGUE: PUSH

Every letter typed here is my fingers' movement away from my hair. At the same time, the spaces in between every word, every sentence, contain the hairs I pulled when gripped by fear of continuing to not say enough or to say too much. Or, that anything I say means nothing for children dying in Palestine and Sudan and Congo as I gratefully-guiltily lie next to you, caressing your head and hands and feet—all there. With my other hand, I pull my hairs gently so as not to stir you. Witnessing genocide has irrevocably changed my motherhood; it is with me when I sleep and in every waking moment that I recommit to you, desperately grateful that you (we) are alive, that you can go to school, that you eat, sleep, and smile. James Baldwin's words become more desperately urgent than ever before: "The children are always ours, every single one of them, all over the globe."

I worry that I've wasted so much of my life wanting, trying, to die that, just as soon as you've cemented my reason to live at all costs, I-you-we will actually die. Maybe in another turn of empire, just as what brought us here to begin with.

As you read this, I will be wondering—worrying—what you think. I hope that, even if you don't understand how you became a part of me, you can forgive me.

Some hairs will give up on me and not grow back. Others will, but return different. My hair won't hold a smooth ponytail anymore—the ones that I used to love my mother brushing my hair into, the ones that I began to need because hair around my face began to make me incurably anxious. At some point my hair will decide to completely give up on growing. Patches of my scalp become smooth and shiny like scar tissue. I will remain marked.

By pulling out all the hair she loved and by writing this, I am my mother's traitor. I am her living and dying lie. I am the shame and guilt that is exhausting, debilitating, to try to heal. It is work.

I work on healing not because I am stronger because of trauma but because I am desperate for relief from pain. And I feel the need to prove that I am worthy of living. So, trained as I was to be a workaholic in pursuit of some semblance of worth and lovability, I committed to a series of projects to mother myself—the work that never ends:

Eat

Not in the way some might think an Asian American woman would. This is not the typical "I cook noodles and now I know myself" story. No cookbook-worthy ancestral recipes here. I come from a line of women who did not exactly love to cook. My mother specifically told me it was easier to buy the food from people who knew how to make it well and that she would show me the best places to go for my favorite dishes. Tangled up in that to-go bag of love were spirals of Yelp lists, then binging and starving with every other wave of depression and suicidal thoughts. Without my mother to share takeout from Little Saigon, food became even more complicated.

To crave in Vietnamese, as I learned it, is "thèm." I craved the simplicity I imagined other people had with food. Simplicity.

Our middle daughter had an uncanny knack for baking since she started practicing it as a pandemic-era toddler. To pique her sharp palate and explore recipe ideas, I took her to sample bánh cam, bánh bo, and chè at bakeries across Little Saigon—some from my childhood and other new ones run by second-generation like me. One was both. Nestled in the corner of a strip mall, Đông Hưng Viên Bakery was as I remembered it, down to the smell of the birds picking at soggy newspapers in the parking lot. What was new was that nobody made a big deal out of my being there and ordering in Vietnamese, and now they offered vegan options of every bánh mì and pâté chaud that I had been missing, that had been making me feel even more distant from the flavors I grew up with. Eager to share these familiar-different tastes with my daughter, we loaded up on mooncakes, xôi, and bánh tiêu. Nothing was lost.

To make us feel at home in flavors even older and simpler, I signed my daughters and me up for classes on how to make bánh chưng. At Alma Farms in Compton, the Bánh Chưng Collective demonstrated how to fold the banana leaves and tie the twine into a little gift of soaked rice around a sun of mung bean paste. Our fingers fumbled around our sloppy squares, so I reassured my daughters that we were continuing a family tradition, that this was in our ancestral spirit. I told them how their great-great grandmother, named Number One (bad luck in numbers from the beginning), made the very same dish steamed in an old trashcan over a fire in the back of her house in Đa Lạt. "A trashcan?" They crinkled their noses. "She did what she could with what she had," I explained to them. They nodded and smiled and shook their heads like they knew her: "Oh, Grandma One," they said. The trashcan is where most of the gỏi cuốn that I taught myself to make at home ends up. One daughter practically drank the extra-limey nước mắm I made in an old pickle jar, but grimaced at the spring rolls with my homemade đồ chua.

It was pickling that helped me work on transforming hate into love. I ate kimchi, measured vinegar and garlic with my tongue that had learned to say untruths. I turned to books and films and podcasts to learn from Korean Americans. *Feeling Asian* with Youngmi Mayer and Brian Park got me through bouts of suicidal thoughts when I had the most to lose. I was naked with Koreans again, but this time at home.

Speak

I worked on learning positive language. I cringed and squirmed when Mike complimented me—"brave," "powerful," "honest"—but gradually harnessed the impulse to deflect every kind word with a neutralizing self-deprecating joke. Instead, I swallowed the sarcasm, however hilarious, and said, "thank you." The hard part of listening is learning to say it in return, and I realized that I did not know these words in Vietnamese, the words that I want to say to our daughters. In this language, I was still a baby.

EPILOGUE: PUSH

So I started learning Vietnamese. Again.

After I switched Duolingo to silent, I found myself lonely for our language. I watched and rewatched Instagram reels by Chris Tran and @cinnaminhtoast whose humor about our Southern accents reassured me that I was, in truth, Vietnamese. And they updated me on the language that, for my mother, had remained arrested at the year she had to leave. But I knew I had to do more than tap on the screen glowing in the night. Signing up for the Southeast Asian Diaspora Project's online course for heritage speakers was scary. There'd been a hot dog incident, but before that there were years of mockery and ridicule for every intonation that I got off pitch, or every honorific I misused because I didn't privilege the patriarchal, or when I slipped in an English word because the stuttering search for the Vietnamese term was deafening. Every week, I logged into class and, even though I surprised myself with being able to read and pronounce the majority of the words, the words I didn't know were positive nouns or adjectives: tự tin (confident), hăng hái (enthusiastic), nhã nhặn (elegant), bình tĩnh (calm). I was ignorant about the vocabulary because all I'd heard were criticisms of myself (and everyone else). My response was to joke with classmates how "this Mỹ lai bitch is triggered" and a barrage of other self-deprecating comments in the chat and unmuted.

My classmates' laughter made it easier to face the elisions in the language I inherited. I became a bit of a class clown among a Zoom room of beautiful, talented diasporic Vietnamese women. Despite my deflections, my cohort saw the taut nerve thrumming under every joke. Toward the end of our eight weeks together, one of my classmates, in all tenderness, said to me, "When you speak Vietnamese, you sound like home."

I had a newfound confidence in my ability to speak Vietnamese outside of the tense miscommunications with my mother. The aunties selling áo dàis at the Phước Lộc Thọ shopping mall praised my Vietnamese and my daughters' ability to understand it, complimenting me by criticizing their own children's inability to speak or comprehend the language. Boldened by these women who didn't know how much I needed them, I even carried on an entire conversation with a man. He worked at Bảo Hiên Rồng Vàng where he sold us bánh đậu xanh, my middle daughter's first request for her birthday party. (So Vietnamese.) I was relieved that he could understand my Vietnamese and that he didn't respond in English but talked to me like we were old friends.

I forced myself to talk. In family, with friends, at work, I was always the listener, but now I had to take up space. I became the co-host of a podcast with a person whose glow and laughter uplifted me just by being with her. We cackled at John Mulaney's line in *Baby J*: "All I could care about was what people thought of me. I don't care anymore. I don't care because I can honestly say, 'What is someone gonna do to me that's worse than what I do to myself?' I'll kill him!" We laughed at shared mental health memes about our anxious attachment styles and overanalysis. On brand, as I told stories and jokes, I still heard the running inner monologue that criticized everything I said and how much I said. I spiraled into overanalysis of everything I did and didn't say, just as I regularly lost sleep kicking myself over verbal gaffes I'd committed as far back as second grade. Then, blackout. Listeners would text quotes from episodes that I had completely erased from memory. Part of my work became the practice of halting the anxiety that every listener hated me, just as my mother did.

I have to keep talking and writing. It's the puzzle that needs puzzling. If I don't, the silence will kill me instead of me killing it.

I'm doing the work of therapy. My therapist looks like Olivia Munn, so of course she makes me angry. Given how us mixed Asian women have only been celebrated if Maggie Q–level beautiful, seeing Therapist #9's face next to mine in Zoom sharpens the painful optics of exoticization. Inescapably part of colonization, I am simultaneously intoxicated and revolted. I don't share this, though. Instead, I just minimize my self view so I can focus on her Munn-perfect beauty, complete with brows, lashes, and white white teeth. I am most uncomfortable when she teaches me that silence not only is the punishment I'm used to it being but can also be a practice of healing. When I log onto our sessions, she does not kill me with the platitudes or pleasantries that both infuriate and deplete me daily with administrators and PTA moms. However, she does allow me to perform the conversational equivalent of picking a scab or pulling a coarse eyelash. Even though I know I'm not supposed to ask her questions as I usually would with my friends and students, I ramble and rant about everything from dogs to Complex PTSD to fill the uncomfortable silence. She lets me. Until, as always, I get tired of talking. Then, in her therapist jiu jitsu, she asks me, "Where do you feel that in your body?" I struggle to quiet my mind enough to focus on my body without punishing it, pulling from it. If I can locate the pain—usually in the triangle that my Tennessee Williams tattoo creates between my hip bones and belly button or in the crescent of muscle under my right shoulder blade or in my tightening throat—Olivia pushes me further: "Can you sit with it?"

The fuck?

"What if you offer that pain up to your ancestors? What if they can help you carry it?"

What if.

Eventually, I understand what I learned by telling my daughters that "practice makes progress." Each time that I located the pain and anger she had caused where it lived within me, I could touch it, hold it-her, and, steadily, let it-her-you go just enough so that it didn't talk for me.

I feel like it's the first time I've told the truth. All the therapists who saw me at different periods of my life never got the whole story; I was playing a game and never cried during sessions. I just sat there, collecting reasons to leave them. But Olivia has broken through.

Move

Like with a baby, sometimes talking is too much or not enough. I had to move.

I had always cried when watching dancers in parades or acrobats at the circus. The tears mingled envy and joy of their freedom of movement.

I walked. I didn't run like escape. I walked. Like freedom.

I signed up for yoga classes at a nearby Japanese garden, in part to avoid the overstimulation of mirrors and smells and sounds that I'd experienced in the few previous indoor yoga classes I'd taken. Outside, I could distract myself from my body and the bodies of others by focusing on the burble of koi fish's searching lips or the rustle of red Japanese maple leaves. I tried to quiet the inner critic burning me for acting like a whitewashed fetishizer of pan-Asian healing practices. With my body softening into its surroundings, I could quiet—not silence, but quiet—my churning anxious thoughts to actually *feel* the instructor's descriptions that initially made me laugh. My vertebrae *were* unzipping. My ribs *could* lift. And the fucking supta matsyendrasana . . . these supine spinal twists wrung. me. out. I unleashed sobs. Then, I was comforted by the symmetry of each move. The pieces fit. Later, I pooped without pain.

The relief of symmetry and release, too, got me over my cringe-gag revulsion to massage. As an extension of Olivia's somatic practices, I forced myself to get naked and was validated by massage therapists who, upon barely touching my slouching neck, shoulders, and back that were tense from years of hairpulling, said, "Oh, geez. Yeah," and went to work. Their neuromuscular digs and rubs hurt then eased the knots of grief and shame and trauma and doubt and guilt and longing and heaviness of carrying my mother's child and my child and my children.

Lightened, I could move. I could get naked. I could be touched, even in my most wounded state. If I could do all of these things, I could *Footloose* against all that I'd been told I was and wasn't, could and couldn't. Just as studies were published about how dancing was more effective at boosting mental health than any other prescribed antidepressant medication (which I hadn't taken since my first battle with postpartum depression), I was holding regular dance parties with you. All that bound me to a mere head bob during the dozens of concerts I went to with my dad unfurled. Lucille Clifton reminded me to dance. I honed my *Thriller* jerk and slide to your squeals of glee, taught you to retro-swim to "Love Shack," and loosed juicy booty bounces to our Beyoncé playlist. Mike brought music into every room of our home, and we followed in dance. He told me, "Joy is rebellion too."

See

Human babies need six months to be able to see the spectrum of colors. Up to two years for full vision.

EPILOGUE: PUSH

This might seem natural, not like something you need to learn. A fat chunk of parenting, though, is pointing and saying "look." You have to teach your baby what and how to see.

I was way behind.

I had spent my whole life desperate to be seen but only getting glimpsed through someone else's lens. The hairpulling only exacerbated my fear of being seen through a filter as absence, as negative. The way I saw myself refracted the way I saw everyone and everything around me.

I had to learn to see myself. I had to see not in the echoes that I was the worse or an idealized projection of myself onto movie stars. I had to look into the phoropter and not focus on my lashes, on what was missing. I had to look away from the estrangement from my mother (which, with the help of Carolyn Huynh's *The Fortunes of Jaded Women*, I reassured myself could be temporary). I had to focus instead on all the family I had chosen and who had chosen me. These are the ones you asked about why you have so many aunties and uncles and cousins; these people (yes, for once, "these people" is a good thing) are all the devastatingly, inspiringly beautiful, smart, funny friends and classmates and colleagues and students. Even though these relationships triggered the paranoia that they all hated me because everything I said was stupid, I pushed myself to reach out to them, asking questions as I was comfortable doing but also offering in return pieces of myself. Things that, if I died tomorrow, they could say they knew me by.

I had to learn what I always tell those students: By being who you are, you do not take away from your culture, but add to it. By embracing the asymmetry of ourselves, we could chip away at the monoliths of "authenticity." If I could see myself, I could resist the disappearing that had been done to our ancestors, that had been done to me in my mother's quickest of comments that I grew "too ugly" to have a birthday party past nine years old—the disappearing that I had been replicating onto myself. Present, I could focus on the moment, on gratitude, even celebration.

Appropriately, it was the year of the dragon that I volunteered to do Lunar New Year presentations at your elementary school. In one, I read a bilingual Tết book to a room of five-year-olds who had my precarious cultural identity in their little hands. The stone in my stomach dissolved when they delighted in learning how to say "*chúc mừng năm mới*" and tapping their laps like lion dance drums. Remember how we made it fun? In the second presentation, I was part of a team of Asian American mothers who shared our respective artifacts and traditions for the new year. I invited your first-grade self up to the front of the room to teach the class how to say "*chúc mừng năm mới.*" Proud, you held up your favorite áo dàis and let your friends touch the soft and silky fabric. You distributed bánh đậu xanh as I told the students how each little cube teaches us to be gentle and grateful, otherwise crumbling to a powder between our fingers. I allowed myself to stand back and take mental pictures of your smiles as we shared our culture with the class. You felt like a part of it, and it was a part of you.

Afterward, the other mothers and I commiserated on how this one-hour presentation salved years of trauma—the iconic stories of being made fun of for our lunches, our names, our language, our difference. Our kids were proud of who they were because we were showing them how to do different. I could see how far we've come.

Although "practice makes progress," there are also backslides. I once taught a lesson on the cyclical structure of Toni Morrison's *Beloved*. The ghost always returns.

My first visit to Hawai'i was a work trip right after my first sabbatical, which I realized most people thought meant I was terminally ill or being punished.

> **Sabbatical** (n.): a specific torture strategy for those who ceaselessly pursue, yet fail to accept, validation by overworking until sick which in turn prohibits the travel that everyone expects you to regale them with upon your return.

I was eager to return to work because it, in a reversal, enabled me to travel. But no matter how hard I tried to be involved on the trip, I felt ineffectual, obsolete. I sunk further into the palimpsest of colonialism, blood on lava rocks. Across the Pacific, you were happy at home with your dad who would always be more fun and loving and safe than me. I was overcome with the feeling that everyone was better off without me. The whole-body sensation was like what a frayed electrical wire looks like, split and sparking. I felt it most urgently as the Pacific waters lapped at the lower crescent of my kneecaps—the only bones we are not born with. The water was warm, just the temperature to match my body's, and so I gradually—almost peacefully—numbed to the electric sizzle inside me. This water that touched both shores that I come from, this water I had spent so much time thinking about and longing for, lulled me in and I edged further into it. So much of what I had read, heard, felt, and written about our Vietnamese diaspora centered the Pacific as a space where we had suffered great loss but also whose tides connected us to our homeland. The water was us. As such, I thought that it would be so easy—almost peaceful—to keep walking into it while everyone and the sun were still sleeping, and I would be warm in it. I could settle into a death more gentle than the slicing, shooting, or car-crashing that I typically envisioned.

This was the insidiousness of mental illness and its chronic suicidal beckonings—it tried to contort and erase the great love for and from all of you in an attempt to lure me into death. It tricked me into thinking that dying was a favor—a gift—to myself and everyone around me.

I admit that I was so close to giving in to the weight of everything I've told you and the things I can't: the weight of a memory of you looking at me slumped at the dinner table and asking, "Mom, will you always be like this?"; the weight of loneliness in seeing everything I want to enjoy with you but can't fully; the weight that my constant running away makes me feel like the ancestors—and you—would be ashamed of my ingratitude. The ocean could carry the weight.

Then, a light breeze blew. It reminded me of the coconut lotion from the ABC Market that I had rubbed into my chest earlier that day, trying to soothe away the very thoughts that were pulling me into the water. The wind reminded me that I was in a body that smelled coconut and liked it and moved to buy it from the nice cashier and then rubbed it in circles on my chest as I did with you when you were babies with a cough that Vietnamese has words to ward away (but not sneezes); this was the same way my mother had soothed me when I was a sick child, and I came to understand that part of wanting to die was wholly about wanting to be cared for—in other words, to live. The wind reminded me that I was now the age of my grandparents—from both Việt Nam and Norway—when they immigrated to the US, an age that reminded me there could still be a whole new life ahead of me. Ushered by wind and memory, I made my way back to the shore, away from the water (at least for now) toward the land where things root, where the giant leaves of the 'ape elephant ear plants compelled me to fall to my knees, humbled by how old the land is and how I can survive as it has.

I've since been reading about nature. I often have to force myself to go outside because it is the only place where my mind and body get a break from all that compels me to pull my hair.

Like how you used to wear t-shirts of wolves howling at the moon and bears pawing at honey-dripping beehives, I read about animals, mostly the ones that have remarkable eyelashes. Even though octopuses sometimes will commit suicide after laying eggs, they are just as hellbent on healing; the cephalopod not only regenerates tentacles but can also spontaneously thrust out new eyelashes to protect itself. The sensitivity of the octopus's suckers is equivalent to our fingertips, tongue, and nose combined (imagine them sucking up my white hairs), and their attunement to their environment enables them to change their skin color and texture to camouflage within minutes. Its unparalleled mimicry is rooted in its sharp awareness of how it is seen in its environment.

Then there is the grandest land mammal—the elephant with its thick, coarse lashes that stretch out in long shadows under the savannah sun. These pachyderms have extraordinary communication by sending sound waves across miles. It makes sense, then, that they remember. The famous Thula Thula herd repeatedly demolished fences in the exact spot that would open a path back to where their matriarch was killed by poachers of the same sort that carved ivory jewelry that my great-aunt Adell gifted me before she died. Maybe she, childless, knew she would have to remind me. Trained to question and doubt myself, I've always had trouble remembering, so I would need the reminders—the photo albums and scrapbooks, the bones.

EPILOGUE: PUSH

Elephant calves suffer without their mothers, often circling her poached corpse for days without eating or drinking; in their love for their mothers, they risk their own lives.

The elephant babies *need* their mothers. Even if she doesn't shade them from the sun fully or accidentally stomps on their trunk in the water, they *need* her. For as much as I longed for mine to be there for me only to discover that she was trapped in longing for her own who was missing hers before us, I vow to break our family's cycle of daughters' pain just by remaining here-present, rooted. Curses don't have to be forever. You will not have to circle my body. You will not have to search or sort.

Elephant matriarchs gestate for twenty-two months. Like the octopus mother, she will die to provide for and protect her family. She will wing out her ears so that the sun shines through their vessel-mapped skin. Her pain will be her power. She will charge.

Just like the elephants that the legendary Trưng sisters rode into battle against Chinese invaders thousands of years ago. Even though people have tried to disconnect you from our heritage because you are mixed, our ancestors are still a part of you. Maybe you don't feel as strong as these epically badass sisters or even as your immediate elders in all that they suffered and sacrificed, but remember: the ancestors don't simply place the burdens of history upon your shoulders; on the contrary, they are always there with you, to help you carry the weight. Offer it to them. If you had the strength to pull this hard for this long, that means that you can push too.

Release your fists and open your palms skyward.

You will learn how to start controlling the types of pain your body feels. One method will add rather than take away from your body. I found renowned Vietnamese American tattoo artist, Dizzy Doan, who is in such high demand that I requested to pitch a tattoo that was scheduled for two years out. During the pitch interview, I was so nervous that my stomach dropped and my words tumbled out of control.

I told him why and was relieved when he smiled and jotted down notes. I knew he understood. "Come eat fruit," our mothers said instead of "love."

Dizzy was able to make the remaining scars on my arms the shiny curves of lychees.

EPILOGUE: PUSH

I am trying to keep traditions while breaking cycles and nourishing possibilities. You, my children, are the mangoes, lychees, and mung beans. "Can I have more fruit?" you ask. Yes. I will learn this as I say it to you: You can always have more. I strive to add, not take away.

I am working to offer more than silence every day by lassoing the voices in my head and rewriting their tired script. When you say you are sad but don't know why, my breath catches in my throat because of the fear of inheritance. I swallow it to revise the words you hear from your mother's mouth: "It's okay to feel sad. It's okay if you don't know why. Just feel the sadness. You can cry. We can talk about it. Or I can just hug you. After you feel it, it will pass. The sadness is only temporary. I'll be here with you the whole time you are sad. I'll be here when you are happy. I'll always be here. I'll always love you. Do you want a hug?"

You always say yes. You know you can ask for more.

It's together that we do the rewriting:

One day you ask me to hold your hand while you're on the toilet; as we squat together, you tell me that we've gotten better at showing love, that you like it. "Good," I say, "because I love you." You respond, "Yeah yeah," smiling in the intimacy of jokes, "you tell us every day."

Voicing the truth becomes more satisfying than pulling any amount of hair.

Your voices swell and fade and get close again as you run and dance free-bodied through the home we have built together. Daily, you witness Dad and I embrace, then yell "Romance!" or "Group hug!" always running toward, not away. You count one through ten in Vietnamese, the rainbow's colors in Spanish, and sing in our language of love, "No, I don't want your number/No, I don't wanna give you mine." It echoes: the resounding promise, the hope, the healing of "No."

As a mother, I am a child again. I'm my younger self from all those moments the camera didn't catch. You are my closest ghost, invisible but present in everything. You are as much as who I am now trying to become. I'm doing this for you and for them and for everyone who comes after. I am trying to rewrite everything for you and, now (finally) *to* you. I am trying to love you too, dragonfruit.

EPILOGUE: PUSH

When mother elephants die, their children are nurtured by the herd—the aunties, cousins, sisters, friends, the storytellers who show them the ways to survive. The child will grow to be one who does the same, strengthened by the knowledge and care gifted to her in grief. My herd—the writers, actors, therapists, teachers, students, friends, women and mothers passing through—showed me pieces of who I was. Without them, I wouldn't have been able to become whole.

Now, as a người Việt-lai Mỹ-daughter-mother-reader-writer-student-teacher, I could return to "viết," which means "to write," and, from certain tongues, sounds like "giết," or "to kill." It all depends on context. Who? How? Why? The answers show that, even though these words sound the same, what I needed to hear was all about living.

I had to listen to begin to understand that I had already been part of herds nurturing others all along. I had to learn that, for years to come, I would be an essential member of the herd for our daughters, as well as people I may not have even met yet. I had to hear the hoofbeats slow and rest, to stay.

I found the words I needed at home. My Mike wrote an epic past-future story about children living on rooftops. In it, there is a line that broke me open like the dawn:

"I am proof that we return as the thing we loved. I am proof that you do not need to die to do it."

ACKNOWLEDGMENTS

It would not have been possible to write any of this without my herd that supports and saves me.

Thank you to the Diasporic Vietnamese Artists Network (DVAN) team for accepting me as Vietnamese American by publishing my posts in the early days of *diaCRITICS* to this memoir today. A special thanks to Viet Thanh Nguyen for his gracious invitation to write for *diaCRITICS*. I am grateful to Minh Vu and this memoir contest's guest judges whom I so admire—Lac Su for teaching me with *I Love Yous Are for White People* that it's okay to be our full selves when telling our stories, and Ly Tran whose *House of Sticks* showcased how to honor our parents through difficult truths.

To Editor in Chief Travis Snyder, Senior Editor Christie Perlmutter, and the Texas Tech University Press team who showed me support and encouragement throughout a publishing process that was new, exciting, and emotional for me.

To the teachers who saw me and encouraged me to write: Ms. Ono (4th grade), Mrs. Smith (3rd and 5th grade), Mrs. Potts (10th grade), Mrs. Ross (12th grade), Erica Fuller, Susan Hansell, and Brian Finney (BA), Ray Zepeda and Tim Caron (MFA), and Lisa Lowe (PhD).

To Stephanie Nozaki for her tireless patience, understanding, and emotional labor invested in my trauma therapy. Thank you for your instrumental role in my healing process, and for gifting me a sense of belonging as a mixed Asian American. I forgive you for being good at what you do AND

ACKNOWLEDGMENTS

looking like Olivia Munn.

My healing process has also been greatly facilitated by Stephanie Foo's *What My Bones Know: A Memoir of Healing from Complex Trauma*, Natalie Gutierrez's *The Pain We Carry: Healing from Complex PTSD for People of Color*, Jenny T. Wang's *Permission to Come Home: Reclaiming Mental Health as Asian Americans*, and *Where I Belong: Healing Trauma and Embracing Asian American Identity* by Soo Jin Lee and Linda Yoon. Thank you to the mental health practitioners creating content that makes accessible the otherwise costly investment in healing from trauma: @drdoylesays, @nate_postlethwait, and Dr. Jennifer Mullan's @decolonizingtherapy.

I am eternally grateful to my Aunties Gena and Leslie for modeling motherhood; my cousins "Beige at Best" Erik, Anna, Kari, Anyssa, Cameron, and Kayanu for their unconditional love and checking in on me when I needed it most; my siblings Vinh and Tien; and my nieces and nephews, for hope and purpose.

To my dear friend Ginny Komenda for walking this pothole-infested cyclebreakers' road with me, and to my sister-from-another-mister Lenna ("Leonard") Odeh, for always listening and laughing to unmake the crazy of the war-torn worlds from which we were born. To Kim and Jason Casem for showing me what family could be.

Thank you to my colleagues for trauma-bonding through workaholism and charitably laughing at my stand-up comedy-pedagogy: To my Academic Cholas—Maria Figueroa, Zulema Diaz, Violeta Sanchez—you have no idea how much it means to me to be included in your group of brilliance, badassery, humor, and love. To Keli Ross-Ma'u and all of the Mana students (special shout-out to our alumni Kat, Alesi, Cam, Dannia, Allura, Tāne, Ray, Cass, Wes, Samantha, Kaila, Kennedy, Raul, Connor, Nani, and the Wong siblings) who grant me daily the privilege and honor to be part of their family—you've taught me how to hug, show love, and be a better teacher, auntie, and mother. To Thao Ha whom I so admire for her powerful leadership and moving writing. To Nery Chapeton-Lamas, Aaron Roberts, and Jim Sullivan for exemplifying the bravery to call out racism and capitalism in the fight for justice and empowerment in education. To Tina Helmstreit and France Cruz, my genius collaborators who have gifted

ACKNOWLEDGMENTS

me the lightness of feeling that I belong.

A special thank-you to Allura Murray-Cruz, my friend, icon, and co-host on the *This Makes Me Uncomfortable* podcast. I am grateful to you for "making good choices" to turn pain into joy by talking story and laughing (loudly).

To Christian Lozada, a talented writer and teacher, for holding me accountable and motivated during the writing of this manuscript. Thank you for teaching me so much about writing, from the days of sitting around the MFA workshop circle to today.

I would like to fangirl on writers who inspired me during this drafting process: Carolyn Huynh, Elaine Hsieh Chou, Aimee Nezhukumatathil, Noah Arhm Choi, Eugenia Leigh, Sigrid Nunez, and, yes, Zachary Levi.

As I wrote this book, it was often necessary to drown out my mental noise with the auditory equivalent of Tiger Balm. So thank you to Sudan Archives and Doja Cat for their empowering artistry, and all the writers, musicians, and singers who created the *Encanto* soundtrack, especially Isabella's tear-jerking refrain of "What Else Can I Do?" Thank you to the podcasts *Feeling Asian* and *Fun with Dumb* for making me laugh-cry and relate in profound ways that have helped heal the inter-Asian hate that history ingrained in me. Thanks, too, to the *Armchair Expert* and *A Cup of Tea and a Chat* podcasts that always make me smile and keep me on the road during those wee-hours-of-the-morning commutes.

To my in-laws, Lyn and Ted, thank you for welcoming me into the safe space of your home and family, and gifting our daughters treasured Grands time.

To my mother, I am grateful to you for all the sacrifice and suffering you endured from my birth to death to our birth to death. I will always be sorry that I am not the daughter and you are not the mother we needed.

Thank you to my dad for always showing up, changing my life with books and movies, traveling with me, and being an awesome gramps who always makes the girls' faces light up.

Mike, I don't have enough words to thank you for always choosing and seeing me. I love your brilliant mind and generous heart. I am your biggest fan, and you make me love and laugh harder than I ever thought

ACKNOWLEDGMENTS

possible. It is my greatest honor to be your partner and enjoy what we've built together—family, traditions, and a home filled with love, music, and cookies.

To our children, thank you for your patience, hugs, and dance parties as I've done this hard work of learning to heal and love myself so that I can be better for you. You are everything. Remember, Mom always comes home.

PREVIOUS PUBLICATION VENUES

"The Root," in *Mulberry Literary*, Issue VI: The Unearthed, May 2023.

"Photo Album 1," originally "Photo Tankas 1," in *Poetry Northwest* 16, no. 2 (Winter/Spring 2022).

Portions of "The White NBA" previously appeared in *Flash Fiction Magazine*, November 2020.

"Dear Rider Strong," originally "To Rider Strong," in *X-Ray Lit Mag*, August 2021.

"Thúy," in *Southern Humanities Review* 54, no. 1 (Spring 2021).

Portions of "Puppeteer" previously appeared in *The Palisades Review*, Issue 2 (October 2023).

"Troll," in *Hash Journal* (June 2021).

Portions of "The Christian and the Quail" previously appeared as "The Christian and the Quail" in *Feels Blind Literary*, Issue 6 (August 2021) and "I Almost Dated a Guy" in *Blood Tree Literature*, Issue 10: Re:Union

PREVIOUS PUBLICATION VENUES

(November 2021).

Portions of "Sleeper" previously appeared as "The Student" in *Michigan Quarterly Review: Mix Tape*, Issue 4 (March 2021).

Portions of "Undercover Gook" previously appeared as "I Dated Another Guy Who" in *Impostor: A Poetry Journal*, Issue 4 (October 2021) and "I Never Dated a Guy Who" in *sin cesar* literary journal, October 2022.

"Photo Album 3" previously appeared as "Photo Tankas 2" in *West Trade Review* (Fall 2020).

"Diem, the Tailor," in *Tabula Rasa Review*, Issue 1 (June 2022).

"Letter to a Mỹ Lai Mother," in *Witness Magazine* 34, no. 2, Fall 2021.

ABOUT THE AUTHOR

Jade Hidle is a Vietnamese-Irish-Norwegian writer and educator. She is a Pushcart Prize and Best of the Net nominee. Her travel chapbook, *The Return to Viet Nam*, was published by Transcurrent Press in 2016, and her work has appeared in *Poetry Northwest*, *Southern Humanities Review*, and *Craft Literary*, among other journals. She was a featured writer on the Diasporic Vietnamese Artists Network's diacritics.org. You can follow her work at www.jadehidle.com or on Instagram @jade_hai_do.

AUTHOR PHOTO BY VIVIAN TRINH THI BUCKLEY